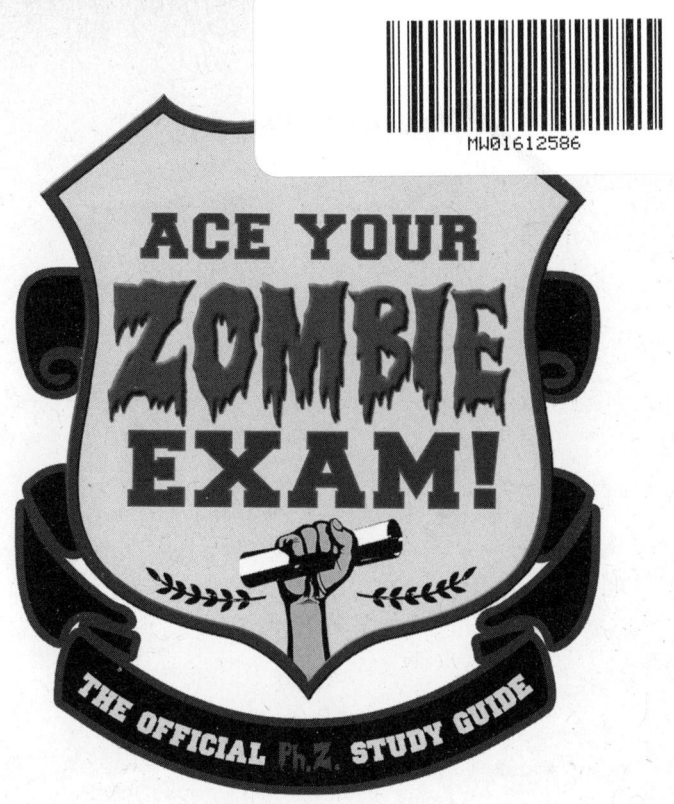

ACE YOUR ZOMBIE EXAM!

THE OFFICIAL Ph.Z. STUDY GUIDE

DAVID P. MURPHY, Ph.Z.

Brought to you by
Exam Services Corporation
and
The Capon Académie
"We'll learn you good!"

Published by Sourcebooks, Inc.
P.O. Box 4410, Naperville, Illinois 60567-4410
(630) 961-3900
Fax: (630) 961-2168
www.sourcebooks.com

Library of Congress Cataloging-in-Publication Data

Murphy, David P.
  Ace your zombie exam! : the official Ph.Z. study guide / David P. Murphy ; additional illustrations by Daniel Heard.
      p. cm.
  "Brought to you by Exam Services Corporation and The Capon Academie."
  1. Zombies—Humor. I. Heard, Daniel. II. Title.
  PN6231.Z65M86 2011
  818'.602—dc23

                            2011033237

            Printed and bound in the United States of America
            VP 10 9 8 7 6 5 4 3 2 1

Also by David P. Murphy
....

*Zombies for Zombies: Advice and Etiquette
for the Living Dead*

*Zombies for Zombies—The Play and Werk Buk: The World's
Bestselling Inactivity Guide for the Living Dead*

CONTENTS

ACKNOWLEDGMENTS

To all the usual suspects, family and friends—much love and gratitude.

And to the folks who've purchased these books and have enjoyed the journey thus far—thank you. I'm just trying to make a few people chuckle.

To Laurie Fox and Peter Lynch—I'm lucky to have the kind of support you both offer.

And, in general, to our educational system—thanks for being such an easy target.

•••

History is a race between education and catastrophe.
—H. G. Wells

To repeat what others have said requires education;
to challenge it requires brains.
—Mary Pettibone Poole

•••

FOREWORD

BY DR. KENNETH BEAKER, Ph.Z.

Welcome to the rest of your life—a place where every decision you make will be correct. Impossible? Not at all—not once you receive your Ph.Z. degree. And you'll do that by passing the Zombie Aptitude Test (ZAT). (You may know it by its interchangeable nickname, the Zombie Exam.)

Like a giant wad of C4, the ZAT is the weapon that will blow the door off your entry into the promised land of your best destiny. (Sometimes the similes write themselves.) But perhaps I overenthuse. I'm passionate about this Exam and, quite frankly, much of the world doesn't understand why.

The reason is simple: I have direct experience with the Exam, having revived it from its own zombie-like state a number of years ago. As a result, I was one of the first people to be awarded the prestigious Ph.Z. In the following decades, the Exam and the Ph.Z. have improved the lives of countless people in ways I can't even begin to describe because (a) the details elude me and (b) many of those people no longer return my messages.

Do you need a little motivation regarding the Exam? Check it out: I've been afforded numerous remarkable opportunities I wouldn't have otherwise had by having the tasty title of Ph.Z. after my name. But perhaps the most exciting one happened last week—I got to shake Carrot Top's hand at a convenience store opening. Have *you* done anything like *that* lately? I didn't think so.

"Jeepers, I'd study anything if I could meet Mr. Carrot Top!"

I'd be remiss if I didn't give major props to the Capon Académie and Exam Services Corporation (E.S.C.). Without their considerable assistance and occasional threats, I'm not sure this Murphy fellow would've finished this book.

Speaking of "considerable assistance," this book doesn't pay for itself, you know. Please support the sponsors whose ads appear herein. If not for them, this guide would've had a harder time finding its audience or a place on any shelf.

Later, after this bloody mess is over with and you're basking in the afterglow of a test well taken, get yourself over to TC's Epstein Bar & Grille. Their "Bowl of Shame" happy hour drink special will make you forget all about the Exam, along with many of your lifelong issues.

There's an old Buddhist proverb that goes something like this: "When the student is ready, the Master appears. And the Master appears to be pissed." I think we all can agree that that proverb resonates here.

Study well, live well, and don't worry—there are no longer any blowfish in the ZAT.

Best regards,
Dr. Kenneth Beaker

A COMMENCEMENT ADDRESS

FROM YOUR PRESIDENT,
President Dutch Bingo

Let me be the first person to congratulate you on getting through your Zombie Exam.

What do you mean they haven't taken the test yet? Of course they have. I only give the speech when diplomas are about to be awarded and they're only doled out once they've taken the test. Got it?

What? Oh. This is the beginning of the book. Well, I didn't know that. Why don't you people keep me informed properly? Damn it.

Ahem.

As I was saying, I look forward to offering you my congratulations later, upon the completion of the Exam. Good luck with your studies.

Sincerely,
Your President, President Dutch Bingo

WHAT'S ZAT YOU SAY?

"Why did I buy this knock-off study guide? I can be such a ditz!"

First of all, everyone at the Capon Académie and E.S.C. would like to thank you for your purchase of this book. We know that when it comes to ZAT study guides, you have a lot of choices—choices like that dippy *All-Night Cram of the Living Dead* or the equally inept *Up Yours—Score, That Is!* We're grateful you didn't buy those guides—they have a success rate lower than a contortionist's nads.

Anyway, humans, zombies, post-lifers—we're not that different. We're all hungry for a better life or post-life, as the case may be, and we're all looking for that one way to get ahead (or "a head," if you will). But most importantly, we all share a common aspiration: being the coolest person in the room!

DID YOU KNOW?

For those of you who may have been unconscious for the last few years, let's review the current terminology:

"Horde": your everyday garden-variety pack of the living dead; another word for zombie.

"Post-Lifers": folks who are sorta dead, but who were able to preserve some of their humanity through Zombies for Zombies products.

"Scarlet Shores": a chain of assisted post-living facilities where the post-lifers are housed.

That's why so many folks are more frequently turning to education in order to improve their station in life and, thereby, up their coolness quotient. And when they do choose this time-proven route, the majority are choosing an option other than your standard-issue Harvard or Yale degrees in passé disciplines like law or business. Instead, they're pursuing the grooviest degree there is—the highly coveted Ph.Z.—and they're doing it *outside* of university walls! No enrollment necessary— you need only this book, a nearby Testing Center, and your own high-octane noggin.

A reminder: the ZAT is *not* the same as the SPLAT (Scholastic Post-Life Aptitude Test). The SPLAT is *only* for the post-lifer population. If you're a post-lifer and you've gotten your "hands" on this book, you need read no further. Your higher education ends at the SPLAT. You're not eligible to receive a Ph.Z. degree; bummer to be you. But do make sure you pick up *Ace Your SPLAT*, the bestselling study guide for the recently bitten. That'll help your cause!

And what of you, Mr. or Mrs. Uninfected Citizen? Do you sometimes feel left behind by the post-Disaster world? Are you jealous of the perks and stamp programs that post-lifers receive? No worries—*now* is the time to pursue your Ph.Z. With this honor under your belt, you'll be exponentially more employable *and* enjoyable, particularly if you can get that aforementioned belt to hold up your chinos.

BUT I COULD *NEVER* PASS THE ZAT.

"When I come up there, I better not find you boys horsing around. You've got to study for your ZAT!"

Pish, posh. This degree is *nothing* like the all too common Ph.D., which can involve years of class work, snory research, and a long-winded thesis your own mom wouldn't read. The ZAT requires that you show up for *one day* at a Federal Testing Center and put in roughly six hours to take the Exam. Stick to the steps listed in this guide and you'll breeze through the sucker and soon take on whatever's left of the world.

HMMMM. WHAT EXACTLY IS IN THIS BOOK?
Inside you'll find:

- ⊙ Valuable suggestions for how to properly study for each segment of the test;
- ⊙ A series of tips where you'll be walked (in some cases, limped) through precisely how to dress, how to act, and where to sit for the big event;

- ⊙ The easiest method for getting a perfect 483 on the Interrogation section and how to nail the dismount; and
- ⊙ The inside scoop on Testing Centers and intel regarding which month practically guarantees that you'll ace the test.

DID YOU KNOW?

- ☛ Over fifty years ago, British expatriate Roland Chestnut devised the first version of the Exam during an overindulgent summer break at the Port-au-Prince Capon Académie.
- ☛ Chestnut's beta group for the test included a local voodoo practitioner, a butcher, a traffic cop, two petty thieves (who'd been zombified as punishment), three teenage fanboys, and a rooster farmer.
- ☛ The first ZAT included a "Blowfish Dissection" segment. Sadly, this was a sign that Chestnut had gone too far and made the ZAT more technical than needed. As the majority of students began to flunk the Exam, interest waned and the test was retired.
- ☛ Thirty years later, a young Dr. Kenneth Beaker spent a semester studying in Haiti and, as fate would have it, wound up at the Capon Académie. Inspired by his love of zombies, he dove into the Académie's archives in order to research his core thesis—"The Living Dead and Home Mortgages: Don't They Deserve the Dream, Too?" One afternoon, he stumbled upon Chestnut's test, as well as notebooks full of mostly coherent thoughts and scribblings.
- ☛ Beaker contacted the Académie's administration and the Gaggle of Governors gave him permission to reinstate the Exam along with the Ph.Z. degree. From there, he tweaked much of the content in order to make it more "tester-friendly."

Best of all, this guide offers a sample test that, once taken, will give every reader an advantage over their test competitors. (FYI: the actual Zombie Exam is much longer and, despite the six hours allotted, typically involves a sweaty race to the finish line.) By drilling down on the segment-by-segment study instructions, you won't be intimidated when the real 2-lb. test booklet hits your desk for the first time.

As you progress through this book, you'll learn how to study for each section of the exam and what each section is worth in the total score:

- Critical Reading (20% of total score);
- Meat (5% of total score);
- Logic & Math (5% of total score);
- Zombie Lore & Movie Trivia (40% of total score);
- Vocabulary (10% of total score);
- Geography, History, & the Social Sciences (10% of total score);
- Interrogation (10% of total score); and
- Ethics (15% of total score). (And yes, that does add up to 115%. Ethics flunked Math.)

I *LOVE* ZOMBIES, BUT MY MATH SKILLS SUCK AND I'M A VEGETARIAN. ERGO, I'M SCREWED.

"Ergo"? Who are you trying to impress?

Ace Your Zombie Exam! The Official Ph.Z. Study Guide will prepare you for the test in spite of whatever deficiencies you may have. By sticking with the book's system, you'll be in a cap and gown in no time flat, with "Pomp and Circumstance" blaring away in a mind-numbing loop. Well, you *would* be in a cap and gown if ceremonies were still held for the occasion.

"Why can't I keep my Romero films straight? It's 'Dawn' then 'Day'!"

And did we mention the blank diploma at the back of the book? No need to wait for your sheepskin to be mailed to you by mail delivery (which has been a bitch post-Disaster). Just take the scissors, cut out your diploma, fill in the blanks, and frame that baby. You've earned it!

OKAY, YOU'VE CONVINCED ME. I'LL START STUDYING TODAY!

Whoa! Slow down there, Magellan. You can't just sail willy-nilly into the process. For example, would you even know the answers to these two sample questions on your own?:

- ⊙ Fedji Wilson and Odette are about to zombitize an acquaintance, a 62-year-old man with a weight of 156 pounds and a height of 5 feet 8 inches. For the zombification, Fedji is leaning toward the coup de poudre, while Odette prefers Datura. Please explain, in your own words, which substance would be the better fit for the ritualistic event and what amounts to use given the acquaintance's physical characteristics.

- ⊙ Jim wants to sell three goats to the voodoo priest who lives down the lane. Should Jim consider selling two and donating one in order to not invoke the wrath of Maurice, the lesser voodoo spirit who resides in the priest's attic, and who has been known to tango in the town square at dusk? Maurice has also made it clear he's fond of lamb every now and then, but Jim has no clue how to read the goat-to-lamb conversion table. List the pros and cons below.

We didn't think so. There are two things true in this life: you don't go into the jungle without a sherpa and you don't study for the Zombie Exam without this book. If you want to ensure your success, fork over the moolah and buy it now. You'll never regret it (but, to be clear, there are no returns).

So, remember: don't let your stupid neighbor get there first. After you finish this book and the sample test, get yourself to a Federal Testing Center and tell 'em—

"I'M GONNA ACE THAT ZOMBIE EXAM!"

FREQUENTLY ASKED QUESTIONS POSED TO THE AUTHOR

SO THERE REALLY IS SUCH A THING AS A PH.Z.? WOW. I THOUGHT THAT WAS JUST ONE OF YOUR DUMBASS GAGS.

I get that a lot. Some people think all I do is make up stuff.

But you heard right: the mighty but once little-known Ph.Z. has become the hottest trend in education today. Why would that be?

As a result of the outbreak of the Provo Virus and the societal downturn that occurred after the Disaster, we're dealing with multiple problems on a massive scale. Among these are a soaring deficit, an erratic power grid, and the public outrage regarding the discontinuation of the McRib. On top of that, the job market sucks and the pay rate for the few jobs that are available sucks even more. And the jobs themselves? C'mon, who wants to do those—certainly not *moi*. Hemo-Glowin technician at an InfusoHut kiosk? Carcass collector? ShuffleCraft mechanic? Are you kidding me? No effin' way.

Because of this, our collective work force and student population alike have become, shall we say, discouraged. The kind of discouraged that leads to keeping a jug of Diet Dew by the couch, playing Farmville for 32 hours a week, and not bathing until late afternoon. But, y'know, those funky folks pose a legitimate question: Why better yourself by pursuing traditional educational pathways if it's not going to get you anywhere? When seen in that light, slacking off is understandable (with the exception of the part where you're playing Farmville).

"I sent those Mafia Wars invites out 2 weeks ago! Why doesn't anyone 'like' me?"

The hard truth is a master's degree, a doctoral degree, or your seventeenth certification in Windows SQL Server 37th Anniversary Platinum Edition Plus will no longer put you in the driver's seat. Almost no one is hiring,

Only 3 out of 8 citizens are currently pursuing the Ph.Z. degree. A sad statistic, indeed.

and you—like me—probably have too much experience for the positions that are out there. And do you really want to be a Quali-Ko™ greeter? I think not.

But what if there was a degree that bestowed sheer grooviness on its owner, like having a paisley aura. Well, that is precisely what a Ph.Z. degree will do for you. This title added to your name tells those around you that you know that they know that you *ROCK*.

Here's how it works: once you pass the ZAT and get your Ph.Z. (and all the "knowledge" that comes with it), you'll be an expert in the one field everyone is talking about—zombies. (Oh sure, we're encouraged to call them the "Horde"—whatever.) Despite the existence of the Containment Zones, freely roaming zombies in our neighborhoods continue to be a bona fide problem. Because of this and the "hangover" from the Disaster itself, *the* topic of conversation at cocktail parties and other social gatherings is "the living dead and what's to be done about them." If you were to suddenly become a zombieologist,

Subject A, aka Doofus— beloved member of the Horde.

you would then be the most interesting (i.e., coolest) person in the room.

"Didja hear? Skeeter passed his ZAT! I am sooooo gonna do him!"

You'd make that Dos Equis guy look like a dweeb. For men, this means gals will fawn all over you. As for the gals, guys love a woman who can actually talk about zombies without rolling her eyes.

According to the federal website, there's currently a nine-week waiting list to take the Zombie Exam, so make your reservations soon (go to www.testing123.gov). Meanwhile, until your slot comes open, dive into this book and get your student on. Nail this dawg and you'll move to the front of the line.

I DON'T REALLY CARE IF I'M AT THE "FRONT OF THE LINE." (PAUSE: LONG SIGH.) ANYWAY, SO WHAT'S CONSIDERED A GOOD SCORE?

Anyone who really cares about their station in life will want to get as close as possible to the perfect score: 4733. That score would include the rarely awarded 83 bonus points for "no sweating" within the Interrogation segment—not easy to do. I've only known other person—besides me—that's gotten a perfect score on her Exam and that was the lovely and talented Gwyneth Paltrow. Looks like I'm in good company!

As stated, the perfect score is difficult but obtainable. And just because it's a long shot doesn't mean you should let up on the accelerator. If you can't get a perfect score, I'd sure like to get you into a perfectly acceptable 4200. Hey, a 3750 would even look good on you. What would it take to get you into a 3750 *today*?

"Like I need your lame program!"

YOU KNOW, I'M SMART AND I LIKE MYSELF JUST FINE. I DON'T HAVE TO TAKE A STUPID TEST TO IMPRESS YOU OR ANYONE ELSE.

Uh-huh. What's cute about that statement is that you believe it. Now, pay attention.

This country, this world, isn't what it used to be. Despite what some would have you think, the Disaster took a huge toll on our civilization that, sociologists say, will impact us for two to three generations to come. The economic and cultural damage is formidable and the Lifetime Movie Network went off the air almost two years ago. In other words, you'll be needing all the help you can possibly get regarding your status, your image, your résumé, your wallet, and—to be candid—*you* in general. Without making the effort to acquire every tool available, my friend, it will be *you* who will be the tool. The Ph.Z. degree is a shimmering Wonka-esque golden ticket to the candy store of opportunity. Okay, maybe it's only silver-plated but it *is* special and it *will* open doors. And there will be candy.

Perhaps now you understand the "why" of obtaining this degree. Or not. Either way, let's take a look at the "what."

WHAT?

I said let's take a look at the "what"—the stuff you need in order to ice this muthuh.

There's nothing to be afraid of—hit that Meat out of the park!

UHHHHH, OKAY...

The Exam had been updated in numerous ways since the Chestnut years and then, in Beaker's hands, became more comprehensive and accessible. And now, under the guidance of Exam Services Corporation, it's finally reached its full potential (or so they claim). You'll find that the questions cover an impressive array of subjects (within a specific zombie framework) and, despite what you've heard, the new "Meat" category can be owned with a night or two of studying and dining. I recently took a supplemental test to keep my degree up to date (the questions are wayyy harder). I was hungover like a mastodon, but zipped though the "Advanced Meat" segment in no time flat.

By the way, if you think you'd enjoy a more comprehensive overview of the history of testing, please refer to Appendix A, "Testing Through the Ages!"

HOLY CRAP, THAT SOUNDS BORING. OH, BY THE WAY, IS THIS GOING TO TAKE MUCH LONGER?

Yes. Next question.

DANG. OKAY, WHAT DO I NEED TO KNOW ABOUT THE FEDERAL TESTING CENTERS?

There are currently nine Federal Testing Centers in our country. Within the continental U.S., it's estimated that there's a Center within a day's drive from anywhere on the map. Okay, it could be a 2-day drive from Montana, but what the hey I think you could spend an entire day in Montana just trying to get to an IHOP.

These Centers not only host the weekly crowds of hopeful Ph.Z. applicants, but also serve as offices for the DMV and city and county governments. Think of it: to be able to take the Exam *and* renew a driver's license at the same location is the ultimate in convenience.

When you feel ready and confident about your command of the subject, locate the nearest Center to you and make a reservation. By checking the Federal Testing Center website (again, that's http.testing123 .gov) and entering your Post-Disaster Zip+12 Code, you can find driving directions, hours of operation, and romantic lodging packages to make your trip even more enjoyable. And make sure you click on the "Free-Ranger Alert" button at the top-right corner of the home page. There you'll get up-to-the-minute reports regarding Horde activity along your proposed travel route.

Or you may choose to call 1-800-ZATINFO. Please keep in mind, though, that hold times are unusually long, if you're able to get through at all. And the operators may not speak your language.

"ZATInfo? Yes, I can hold."

I'VE HEARD THE PROCTORS CAN BE TOTAL D-BAGS. ANYTHING I NEED TO KNOW THERE?

I must admit, there's a degree of truth to that rumor. Having said that, you need to understand that the Proctors deal with all types of people taking the Exam, many of whom are colossal d-bags themselves. Like multiplying two negative integers, it takes a d-bag to nullify a d-bag. It's a law of the universe.

The reality is, the Proctors have to be prepared to deal with anything, therefore they can seem a bit edgy and tightly wound—one might even say paranoid. (And, to be fair, those six hours in the Testing Chamber— plus your one break—can feel like an eternity.) So, if you *must* engage any of the Proctors on a one-to-one basis (which I would avoid if possible), try not to look directly into their eyes. They frequently take this as a sign of confrontation, and what could follow could be painful or crippling for you.

WHAT ABOUT THOSE OTHER FOLKS TAKING THE TEST? CAN I PARTY WITH THEM?

What are you—15? I know you'll be amongst a number of newfound peers and peeps, but that's not the cue for you to start hanging out in the hotel hallways or comparing notes on using everyday makeup to craft a dynamite facial wound for under five dollars. No, you're not going to "party" with them—you're going to stay sober, get a good night's rest, and be ready for the test.

This isn't a social studies midterm—this is the freakin' ZAT.

Worthington spent the night before the Exam whooping it up and then failed the test the following day. Don't let this be you!

YOU'RE KINDA DRAMATIC.

You don't even know.

But I'm serious: if you put in the time to work this study guide and simultaneously commit to renting as many zombie films as possible, then you should be a shoo-in for the glorious world that awaits you.

"GLORIOUS" SEEMS LIKE A STRETCH.

Whatever. Maybe you could take that energy you expend on making light of this process and use it instead to constructively prepare for the Exam. Possibility?

PROBABLY NOT.

Okay then—that's enough of dealing with you.

BUT...

To everyone else: You think you know your meat and ethics? You're relatively sure your zombie history chops are exceptional? Then forge on, future student—your degree awaits you!

And don't let me down. I've got a lot riding on your success.

CAREERS GALORE!

(WHAT TO EXPECT FROM YOUR FUTURE)

This message is for graduates only!

Once you complete your studies, ace the ZAT, and get your degree, you'll be eligible for many different positions in the private or public sectors, such as:

DEATH COACH

Now *this* is a career with a bright future! The services of Death Coaches are in demand more than ever and *you* could be a part of this top-tier opportunity. With an ever greater number of post-lifers out there, significant needs exist for properly trained individuals who can guide the not-that-deceased onto an appropriate "path of purpose" and into an occasional restroom. Death Coach counseling makes the lifers' stays at the Scarlet Shores facilities much easier, enhanced by generous doses of Romerin-2®. With the recent announcement of a government pilot program that will issue "Therapy Stamps," you'll have a guaranteed income. FYI: Death

"I've had it with Life Coaches! I'm calling a Death Coach tomorrow!"

Coach certification is closely linked with the Ph.Z. program, so those candidates who pass the Exam *will* be given first consideration.

What's that? You've never heard of Death Coaches? Well, why didn't you say so?

A potential client will seek out a Death Coach because said client is having issues regarding uncertainty or may be dealing with physical and/or spiritual listlessness (whereby a client's spirit is literally listing to one side). In the worst cases, there's severe moping and minimal movement. Once an agreement has been reached, the Death Coach and client meet at a semiprivate, secure location to discuss the client's vision and long-term unrealistic goals. Next, the two put together a "Post-Life Game Plan" that will steer the client toward more reasonable vocations such as Badminton Instructor, Cafeteria Lump, or Stamp Changer at the QCasino™.

Death Coaching sounds swell, right? Here's where it gets even more swollen: now regular uninfected humans, or "Reggs," are also starting to deal with sobering issues regarding everything from the Disaster to how the hell the country ever elected a dope like Dutch Bingo. Because of this, we're witnessing an unusual trend: the Reggs are beginning to contact Death Coaches for their counseling needs, eschewing the services of the nebulous Life Coach community. This development is, no doubt, due to how overwhelmed our health care system is and to a shortage of traditional therapists, many of whom continue to be on benders. The newfound popularity of Death Coaches means the client base will continue to grow at astounding rates because the effects of the Disaster aren't going away soon. Those could be good years for you, you Death Coach you!

C.R.U. COMMANDER

Unlike many public service organizations, the Carcass Retrieval Units do not promote from within but, instead, actively recruit Ph.Z. graduates for their Commander positions. They do this because Ph.Z'ers, as a result of their studies, are simply better informed about the living dead. This makes for Commanders who are tactically superior to your everyday Joe. And did you know that C.R.U Commanders *never* do any of the grunt work and have minimal interaction

"C'mon lads, we've got a buttload of carcasses to move today!"

with the carcasses? Yup. Matter of fact, much of the work can be done remotely. Commanders simply connect to the C.R.U.'s virtual private network to oversee operations and assign missions to their given unit. It's as easy as an organ-meat pie.

STAMP ALLOCATION DIRECTOR

With all the federal stamp categories currently in place, our nation continues to seek qualified applicants to help negotiate this massive (and costly) program. The benefits alone make this job worth looking into—four weeks of vacation after the first year of survival, sick (and bite) days galore, free medical *and* dental *and* unlimited stamps for you (with discounts available for your immediate family). Please understand that one of your duties includes frequent visits to the nearest Scarlet Shores facility to determine the efficacy of stamp levels there. The in-house visits can be dicey, but, statistically speaking, there's a low probability of anything awful occurring.

"I'm tellin' you, Scooter, I can totally see myself being a Stamp Allocation Director."

A MEMBER OF THE BOARD OF DIRECTORS FOR THE POST-LIFER OLYMPICS

Until recently, just the idea of an event called "The Post-Lifer Olympics" would have caused an uproar, with critics labeling it idiotic or possibly even criminal. But now this every-other-year extravaganza is a popular draw in our country.

Client 419 attempts to top his personal best of 2 feet 3 inches.

These summer games are where the used-to-be best and brightest gather for a full two days to compete for the coveted Gold Decals. With events such as the Whiffleball Shot-Put, the 10-Meter Dash, and Super T-Ball Extreme, fans and participants alike get all the excitement they can handle. As a graduate, you'll be qualified to sit on the Board, which is an extremely prestigious position, involving almost no responsibility and, quite frequently, free lunches. The last person I knew on the Board scored a two-year stint where her sole chore was to order the prized Decals.

Please take note: with certain sectors of the population and the media starting to push for spending cutbacks, there's a slight chance the Olympics may one day be cancelled. Keep in mind, though, that much of the funding comes from corporate sponsors, so the cutbacks may not impact the games so much. Fact is, there aren't many feel-good opportunities anymore and the corporate sponsors will do their best to keep this one in place.

ZOMBIE EXAM CONSULTANT

Because of the popularity of the Exam, an entire cottage industry has developed around tutoring potential candidates (and writing books about how best to tackle the Ph.Z.). Exam Consultants can charge handsomely for their services, and don't say I told you so, but it's relatively easy to get work under the table. However, you will *not* be allowed to do business with a lifer, unless you want to be a SPLAT Counselor.

● ● ●

The jobs cited above are but a few of the incredible employment opportunities waiting for you after you graduate. The good news is, due to the crumbling of society in general, phresh jobs are constantly being created by the Employers Incorporating Employees into Opportunities Act (The EIEIO Act) and those newly spawned jobs wait in the wings for those who pass the Exam. The post-ZAT/Ph.Z. world will be far different than your dismal prior life. The before and after will rock your socks off.

Now, it's time to take a hard look at the different segments of the test. But first, a commercial endorsement.

THE EXAM SEGMENTS
OR
HOW NOT TO PULL OFF YOUR FACE

Experience has shown us that keeping your composure during the Exam will ensure that you don't blow an "O" ring. By staying cool and taking the long view, you can work through the sometimes-monotonous nature of the test.

"Now remember—no more pulling on your face or those stitches will pop!"

Let me tell you a story. When I was in my late teens (this was well before the Disaster), I had to take my SAT, which was a different kind of tedious beast. I arrived that day an eager student anticipating a bright future, but I left a broken whelp. What happened during the test that impacted me so profoundly? Two things: (a) abject boredom, and (3) the realization that I'd been on the wrong path for quite some time. You see, I'd spent my entire scholastic career working hard, getting good grades, and preparing for that Big Test. Then, when the test arrived, I looked around the room, observed my fellow classmates, and thought, "Holy bejeesus, what a bunch of dorks! Is *this* who I am?" In my epiphany, I could see that, sure, a lot of these folks would probably go on to do better things than I would, their lives defined by success, happiness, and family. But where was the fun in *that*? And with that realization, all the air went out of me, like a sad punctured outdoor inflatable holiday sno-globe. Disillusioned, I spent the rest of the time connecting the remaining dots on the answer sheet.

Why would I tell you such a thing? Quite simply, the ZAT, while daunting and occasionally nerve-wracking, is *not* unbelievably dull like the SAT. Far from it. The ZAT contains relevant real-life material that could make or break you in a dangerous encounter. It also provides information that, when used correctly, could dazzle a complete stranger, making you even *more* popular. Frankly, you don't know how good you have it. I had to do *algebra*, for God's sake!

And another thing: much has been made of the six-plus hours that the test soaks up. But—and I urge you to pay attention here—the time quickly flies by and many testers don't complete the Exam. Consequently, watch the clock obsessively while you're taking it and be as thoughtful with your answers *as time allows*.

Here, a young Herbert Hoover is seen studying for his ZAT Exam.

So, how will a Ph.Z. be beneficial to your life? When's the last time someone asked you who the cinematographer was on *Zombie Strippers* and you boneheadedly said, "Sven Nykvist?" (And you were *so* not even close.) Why suffer through such embarrassment again if you don't have to? You shouldn't and won't.

But in order to get the most out of your shot at the sheepskin, you need to understand where the Exam *itself* is coming from. Get in the Exam's head—think like it and eat like it.

EXAM SERVICES CORPORATION.

Many moons ago, the popularity of the Exam forced the Capon Académie to abandon the Beaker version. This was because, every year, that version of the test was the same. This led to some less than honest behavior among the testees. Because of this, the Académie chose to have the Exam reimagined by an educational marketing and development business named Exam Services Corporation (E.S.C.). Certain traditionalists called this decision intrusive and inappropriate, asserting it was wrong for a corporation to write a test of any kind for an institution of higher learning. The Académie begged to differ, stating that this type of outsourcing had been done at other schools. Furthermore, the Académie claimed that the impartial nature of a third-party series of revised Exams would benefit all. E.S.C. would create a new Exam (with multiple versions) under the strict guidelines and supervision of the Académie. There were questions at the time regarding how E.S.C. was awarded the contract, but none of the charges stuck, not even the one about the congressional page and the voodoo harem. (That was hot!)

DID YOU KNOW?

The team from E.S.C. that devised the new Exam is made up of business leaders, economic advisors, and the occasional teacher. This passionate group spent an entire spring assembling various incarnations of your upcoming Exam. Some students claim the new Exam is harder than the original, while others respond favorably to the addition of cute captioned pictures. FYI: E.S.C. has a unique way of doing things, i.e., their writing style can be insufferable and their questions obtuse. You've been warned.

Before we drill down on specifics, there's one last aspect of the new Exams you should know about—ads. Please don't get derailed by the fact that there will be an advertisement or two during your Exam. Read 'em or don't—E.S.C. gets paid either way.

What follows next are the various categories or "segments" from one of the most recent versions of the Exam. Of course, like me, I'm sure you want to get to the most fun part of the text—Zombie Lore & Trivia. But we have to examine *all* segments.

ETHICS.

If our society is ever going to get back on that pony of civilized behavior and learn to ride again, our citizens would be well served to develop better *morals*. With this in mind, the short essays in the Ethics segment are designed to help you understand the difference between right and wrong, good and evil, and cotto and Genoa salami. The Ethics part of the Exam may seem dense at first, but your responses to these essays are, ultimately, a way by which the Grading Council determines your suitability for the degree.

By the way, the Grading Council is a 13-person panel that, like a bunch of Dan Brown characters, assembles covertly nine times a year in order to verify test scores. Generally speaking, the panel is comprised of a balance of older cranky citizens who don't understand why there even is a Ph.Z. and twenty-something slackers who still wish Phish would have more reunion concerts.

Each essay will be followed by a blank space on the page. Do *not* doodle there. Please *do* give each essay your thoughtful consideration and write your answer in that blank space. And, when doing so, it's advisable to avoid using words like "whatever" and "moronic." Also, when it comes to the views of highfalutin philosophers and their patronizing ethical beliefs, don't flaunt whatever knowledge you have regarding Socrates, Aristotle, or those other hosers. No one cares—just stick to answering the questions in the most matter-of-fact and personal way. Quoting *any* of the Greeks will get you all jiggy with demerits like nobody's beeswax.

Here's an example from the Exam:

> *Your friend Shanice, who can be fun at times when she hasn't been hitting the Loko so hard, has a number of highly offensive names for zombies, like "fleshhead," "stiffy," "feverface," and "deadsack." How do you go about convincing Shanice that no group within our society should endure such demeaning nicknames? And why are you still friends with her? She's such a dim-witted creep. Explain that!*

Gosh, I have to laugh—I'd never heard the term "deadsack" before. That's a good one!

Anyway, what you'll want to do here is reflect deeply on that paragraph and compose a reply that most accurately reflects your position. Is Shanice indeed a creep or simply one more person who's ignorant to the plight of the living dead? Think about it and respond to the best of your ability. And maybe then some.

LOGIC AND MATH.

Logic and Math have been combined in the ZAT because, for the most part, both subjects are mostly irrelevant now. I mean, when everyday actions involve stuff like landmining your lawn, checking the Net for Horde activity, or figuring out the best way to arm your family with trowels, Logic and Math tend to take a back seat. Like a 1950s Mississippi public transportation kind of back seat.

Nonetheless, these 2 subjects are included in the Exam so that the more stodgy members of the Grading Council can determine that you've got at least *something* on the ball. The questions will be multiple-choice and, as always, a few of the answers are inane. Don't worry—as far as the math goes, it's highly unlikely you'll come upon any *true* equations. This segment definitely falls on the "lite" side. Lite is better, right?

For example:

Quadrant A of a Containment Zone holds 340 Horde members while Quadrant B currently holds 512. How many of the stiffies will need to be transferred from one quadrant to the other in order to make the populations equal?

a. Who cares? They're the Horde.

b. Transfer 86 from B to A to even 'em out, but be careful when you do it because, if it's shedding season, them suckers are slippery.

c. A Containment Zone isn't a Testing Center Inn. Dump all the fleshheads into one quadrant—done!

    d. What's next—hire Temple Grandin to figure out a kinder way to round them up? Get a grip.

See what I mean? Not an equation to be found. But it's sort of a trick question because it seems like math, but it's really logic. Sneaky.

There's only one answer that makes sense and it's c. At first blush, you might get distracted by math and think the correct answer is b., but why would anyone ever authorize the transfer of Horde members from one quadrant to another? I mean, c'mon!

VOCABULARY.

Chestnut and Beaker, the founding fathers of the Exam, were passionate about how important a strong working vocabulary is for individuals, particularly zombie fans. And when they first devised the ZAT, being a living dead enthusiast was *not* the cool thing it is now. Back then, most people believed such adoration was weird or childish. Were *they* ever wrong!

DID YOU KNOW?

That book that's under one leg of your cheap computer desk, keeping the poorly assembled thing in balance, is what's called a "Thesaurus" and it was a gift from your parents about a decade ago. Here's a study tip: replace that book with a different book, and open the Thesaurus. Wow—there are all kinds of words in there, huh? Use that book to learn those supercilious words because the Exam will try to grind you about words exactly like *supercilious*.

Let's take a look at a sample question from the Vocab segment:

"As his fever spiked, Cap'n Ash stopped talking and fell backward onto the daybed and into a *paroxysm* of coughing." In this sentence, *paroxysm* means _____?
a. bundle
b. sudden attack
c. celebration
d. introductory period

This one's easy because c. and d. are plain stupid. And "*bundle*" isn't much better—you can't bundle coughing. Weak! That leaves us with b.—*sudden attack*—which sounds about right.

GEOGRAPHY, HISTORY, & THE SOCIAL SCIENCES.

Fortunately for you, like the rest of the Exam, the problems in this grab bag of a segment only relate to these subjects *within* a zombie setting. So, regarding History, there won't be any Archduke Ferdinand references, or anything about the Crusades or junk like that. But be on the lookout for crud about Columbus because he and Haiti go way back. Which was a *complete* drag for Haiti. (The guy would *not* stay away!)

Again, questions will be multiple-choice—you know the drill. Here's a sample to whet your whatever:

A researcher named Zora Hurston may have witnessed the first modern Haitian zombie back in 1937. Villagers claimed a dead gal had croaked thirty years prior and, remarkably, she was still up and at 'em, albeit a bit slowly. What the eff?

a. There's probably a very logical explanation. Maybe she simply dozed off. Maybe she went on holiday. Those villagers can be so naive.

b. Hurston had been hitting the local libations hard and was whacked out of her skull.

c. The info I found on this indicates this gal was a primitive performance artist who went by the name of "Femme Mort." This, of course, translates to "dead woman" and *not* "Mort the woman." Apparently she had quite the act for her time and believed Hurston to be a casting agent.

d. That gal was a zombie and she'd been wandering around for 30 years. How cool is that?!!

I'll be honest with ya—this one's difficult. I'm lovin' c., the performance artist answer, but it sounds too "Dada" for Haiti at that time. Of course, a. and b. seem banal, so that must mean it's d. How pedestrian.

Whatever you do, don't get freaked about this segment—it's not worth many points. And if you *do* happen to get Columbus questions, remember that he was a tool of the highest magnitude. Answer accordingly.

CRITICAL READING.

The Critical Reading segment is a steep climb, but doable. It consists of different "passages." Each passage will be an extended paragraph or two and will almost always begin with a main point expressed in the first sentence. From there, the E.S.C. authors usually make a secondary point that tries to obfuscate the first point with rambling language and pricey words. Don't let that throw you off-course. Mumble to yourself as necessary and no one will notice if you quietly curse.

This snippet illustrates their scummy tactics:

> *"In our society, there's a growing belief in the theory that the Disaster began as a result of an accident involving pizzas. Where do people get ideas such as this? Pizza is a wholesome food with many wonderful qualities such as sauce, cheese, and, quite frequently, a form of meat. The idea that a pizza could ever do you harm is simply silly. Here's an interesting fact: the first pizza in America arrived on a delivery ship in the late 1700s."*

See what the Exam did there? It talked about the Pizza Delivery Accident (which is now of public record) and then moved the reader away from it, choosing instead to discuss the positive qualities of pizza and its history. This is exactly the kind of crap the Exam pulls all the time—it gets you focused on one thing and then arbitrarily switches gears. It's maddening but, once you know its tricks, you can beat it at its own wicked game.

Let's look at another example:

> *"Ever since the Outbreak, illegal immigration has declined in both the U.S. and Canada. It seems that not nearly as many hard-working foreign-born folks are willing to look for a better life picking lettuce and strawberries when the free-ranger threat is still perceived to be out of control. This shortage of workers has made it difficult for certain farmers to recover from the economic impact of the Outbreak and has led to calls for post-lifers to be placed in the fields in exchange for the stamp programs they receive. Did you know that the remarkable drug Productiva® could give post-lifers the level of energy necessary to work in those fields? Isn't it good to know?"*

Okay, what the *hell* is going on there? That passage is all over the road. It begins with an interesting point about how the nature of illegal immigration has shifted, but then ends up selling itself out by hawking a drug. This is a perfect illustration of the Exam *deliberately* trying to

(1) throw you off, and (d) underwrite itself with a bit of not-so-subliminal advertising. None of this existed until E.S.C. came into the picture, but it is what it is. The best thing you can do is embrace the malarkey and move on.

"Oh Pan, I'm so tired of studying! Let's have a chat about those grapes on your head."

Keep in mind that it's important *not* to skip around in the Critical Reading section. As it progresses, the passages become more difficult, as do the questions relating to them. The initial questions may seem simple, but don't get fooled—a massive load of hogwash awaits you.

MEAT.

You can't be an expert on zombies without knowing your meat. (Get your minds out of the toilet, pervs.) You wouldn't go huntin' for whitetails without a big bottle of deer urine, would ya? Of course not. That's why you need to sharpen your wits concerning the living dead's carnivorous culture. As the Buddhists say, "The entrée of my enemy is my friend" and, dang, those Buddhists are right!

Meat questions will be multiple-choice and each more delicious than the last. As always, at least two of the wrong answers are beyond dumb so you'll have a 50-50 shot. I like your chances!

Let's try one:

Horde members are fed an austere diet consisting of a foodstuff that resembles a thick black Manwich. Along with wood chips and other fillers, what two meats are used in this mixture and what are the percentages of each?

a. Beef parts 14 percent and turkey giblets 12 percent

b. Veal 19 percent and bologna 15 percent

c. Chicken skin 9 percent and various hooves 10 percent

d. Fish scales 18 percent and bison lips 18 percent

In checking out the answers, you can see that a. and b. are preposterous. Why? Real beef, even just "parts," would *never* be used to feed the Horde. Also, in regards to b., veal is virtually nonexistent. Duh. That leaves c. and d. Reconsider c. Be aware that, post-Disaster, most available hooves are used to make the gooey substance utilized to repair Containment Zone fences via SuperPluggo launchers. Therefore, hooves wouldn't likely be in the mix, either. That leaves d., which fits because fish scales, when combined with other delectable detritus, can easily pose as meat. And bison lips are tastier than you'd think. Not so hard, huh?

ZOMBIE LORE & TRIVIA.

Now we're talkin'!

Although this *is* the frosting on the Exam cake, don't be lulled into a false sense of security about this segment. Chances are, you don't know as much about zombie trivia as you think you do. The questions are formidable and capable of doing you great damage. When studying for this segment, don't limit yourself to only the last 10 years of zombie culture, go back much farther if you know what's best. Those E.S.C. writers are liable to bring up anything.

It's the same format—multiple-choice.

> *Nzambi* is a word that comes from the Kikongo language, still spoken in certain parts of Africa. In the 19th century, many slaves were taken from those areas and wound up in America and the Caribbean. *Nzambi* is a word for what?
> **a.** pie
> **b.** god
> **c.** brain
> **d.** hat

Hey, E.S.C.—can a student get a little *context*?

Anyway, as usual, two answers—"pie" and "hat"—seem anemic and, I think, show a true lack of effort on the part of the E.S.C. staffers. "Brain" would be an interesting answer, but we'd probably be deluding ourselves to root for it. It turns out the correct answer is indeed b., "god," which makes the most sense because, like our word, "zombie," *nzambi* refers to something greater than ourselves.

Remember: this segment accounts for the highest percentage of your total score. Read each question carefully and try to steer clear of choosing answers you *want* to be correct. Dig deeper, for thy future hangs in the balance.

THE LIGHTNING ROUND.

This is the last written portion of the Exam and your *only* chance to improve your final score. Not surprisingly, the degree of difficulty for these questions is amped up.

Your sample awaits:

Toward the end of the credits of *Night of the Living Dead*, there are images of a group of hunters doing what to zombies?

a. Giving them a two-minute head start.

b. Setting fire to a pile of them.

c. Hosting a lavish buffet.

d. Obtaining contact information.

Any zombie-phile worth his weight in innards knows the correct answer is b. This question does, however, demonstrate what I'm talking about with the Exam: it's not enough to *know* the subject. You better know the subject behind the subject as well as the people behind the history behind the subject. Meeting a few of their relatives would even help. References to background images during the credits? This shit is deep.

INTERROGATION.

Know this: there's no studying for the Interrogation.

Upon completing the written portion of the Exam, you'll quietly close your test booklet and press the green button on your desk. This will signal the two Proctors that it's time to escort you into a nearby empty conference room where four chairs and a small table wait for you. Sit in the single chair that's been placed across the room from the other three.

Your three Examiners will subject you to roughly 20 minutes of intense questioning. This grilling can involve any topic—from why a Ph.Z. degree is important to you to your personal opinion on why Bill Murray was even in *Zombieland*. Try to be as honest and sincere with your responses as possible. The Examiners will look for any signs of fakery and, if found, are authorized to taze you, bro.

It is the wish of the Ph.Z. Authorization Committee that the degree only be awarded to those who are genuine in their love of and commitment to zombie culture. Therefore, should the Examiners, for any reason, find you wanting in character or believe you to be a *poseur*, they have it in their power to deny your application for the degree, even if you excelled in the Exam. Not only that, if the Examiners find you offensive for any reason, they may call in the Bouncers to have you removed from the Testing Chamber.

What else *not* to do? Many applicants attempt to suck up to the Examiners by complimenting their suits and dresses or saying flattering things about the facility itself. Others ooze charm and seek to sweet-talk their way into a degree. This is *not* a reality TV show, folks—this is real. Generally speaking, faux sincerity is met with a swift, strong jolt. You're not in a beauty pageant either—defend who you are, defend your passion for the living dead, and don't let the Examiners get inside your head, because, oh buddy, they'll try. If you honestly believe that any remake of a Romero film (by anyone other than Romero) has been worth a damn, explain why you believe that's true (but do it quickly because those Examiners get itchy trigger fingers). Trust me: if you're the genuine article, you *will* be recognized. It's precisely because getting a Ph.Z. is so freakin' cool that these sorts of steps have to be taken. If *everyone* got the degree, it wouldn't be so exclusive.

In sum, when the Proctors show up to take you to your Interrogation, breathe deeply, center yourself, and try not to soil your NASA diaper. As stated, if your motivations are pure, chances are good you'll come out of the Interrogation unscathed. If your motivations aren't so pure, it may be a very long 20 minutes and, in the worst case, there could be waterboarding.

●●●

Following this brief message, we'll take a "study break" and read a dandy little story about the first few hours of the Outbreak. And then, hold onto your hats because we're going to examine how to behave and what to do prior to and on the big day of the Exam. The anticipation is even starting to get to me!

Let's stretch our legs, get a breath of fresh air, and read a good story. Too bad we don't have one! I kid.

Hey, how about a snack to go with this? How about a pizza?...

STUDY BREAK: DAY 1—INFECTION HO!

∙∙
∙∙

"I'm tellin' you, that pizza is funky. I'm not eating any more of it," Katie said. She made a face as she pushed her plate away, having taken only a bite. "And it's not just the awful ham and pineapple combo."

"Tastes fine to me. I like this combo—it's the Don Ho!" Mark replied. He grinned and took another slice from the box.

Katie was correct, but the pizza was far more than funky. The delivery kid who'd left the young couple's home minutes before had been infected several hours ago by a powerful man-made virus, one that had spread without the kid's knowledge. He'd made a stop to drop off two pies to a nearby lab that conducted tests for a well-known chemical conglomerate. There, he'd been purposely contaminated as a part of an experiment. The scientists at the lab were creating a minor outbreak—"a controlled burn," as they said—of this virus. Once the infection "took," the scientists would arrange for a special anti-viral squad to swoop in, knock it out, and everyone would look like heroes. This effort could very well ensure their funding for years. With the delivery kid's infection, the controlled burn had officially begun, the clock was ticking, and Katie and Mark were merely two of multiple subjects in a six-block radius.

Getting up from the table, Katie walked into the kitchen, opened the fridge, and looked for something else to eat. Pushing aside a stack of takeout boxes, she grabbed a small carton of yogurt, closed the fridge, and pulled a spoon from the drainer. As she dug into the creamy yogurt, her stomach churned. Maybe the yogurt will help, she thought as her mind wandered while standing at the sink.

Mark and Katie had been married for three months and this was their second full week in their new house. The occasional packing carton still lingered in the hallway and in the back of the dining room but, for the most part, they were nearly done unpacking. Katie was anxious to start cooking again—that way, they wouldn't be ordering in so much and could eat healthier.

Mark's violent coughing in the dining room snapped Katie out of her reverie. "You okay in there, hon?" she asked. "Did you accidentally swallow an entire pineapple?" she jabbed.

The coughing continued and she heard a crash. Katie bolted out of the kitchen and into the dining room where she found Mark on the floor wheezing and writhing.

"Mark! What happened? Do I need to call 911?"

Shaking his head "no," Mark quieted his cough, exhaled heavily and whispered, "Yeah, very funny about the pineapple. I think something went down the wrong tube. And you were right—that pizza's weird."

As she grabbed his arm and helped him up, Katie noticed that her husband had a fever. "What the hell, Mark? You're burning up. Should we get you over to the E.R.?"

"No, I'm fine. Let me just get to the couch, okay? The Super Bowl is starting in a few minutes."

Katie helped her husband onto the couch. Hurrying back to the kitchen, she grabbed a dishtowel from the drawer, ran cold water over it, and wrung out the excess. She offered the towel to Mark, placing it on his forehead.

"How are you doing now?" she asked.

"I think I'm a little better. So damn weird—I have no idea what happened. One minute I'm thinking about how the ham has a metallic taste to it, the next I'm down on the floor, trying to catch my breath."

Rubbing his cheek, Katie said, "We've got to get your fever down. And where did that come from? Has someone at work been sick?"

"I don't know. One guy in my department was sneezing like crazy the other day," he replied.

"Let's get some aspirin in you," Katie said. "And I think we *should* get you to a doctor."

"Just give me time to try to feel better, K. It's the Super Bowl. Let me close my eyes and concentrate on relaxing my body," he rasped.

"Alright. I'm going upstairs for the aspirin. Don't go anywhere." She flashed him a weak smile.

"Yeah, right," he said, nodding with his eyes closed.

As Katie walked upstairs, she realized her stomach had gone very far south; she was feeling like she needed to heave. In all the excitement with Mark, the adrenaline rush must've distracted her from her own nausea. She ran for the upstairs bathroom and barely made it to the floor in front of the toilet before she began to vomit. After several moments, she lifted her head from the bowl and sighed. Good grief, she thought. She started to stand and a second wave hit her, forcing her back to her knees. Katie felt as if every ounce of fluid in her system was trying to escape at once.

Flushing the toilet, she remained on the floor for a moment to collect herself. Crap, Mark's down there alone, she thought. Pushing herself up, she looked in the mirror and noticed how heavily she was sweating. Alarmed, she grabbed several Tums from a bottle on the vanity and began to chew. She felt a little bit better, but her stomach was still cranky. What the hell was in that pizza? she wondered. She splashed cold water on her face, opened a nearby aspirin bottle, and took out six—three for each of them—and headed for the stairs.

Katie gripped the handrail firmly, struggling to right herself as she wobbled down the staircase. "Mark, I'll be right there," she called out. "I got sick, too, but I'm okay." She hobbled into the kitchen, grabbed a bottle of water from the fridge, took her three aspirin, and headed into the family room. "Alright, sit up a bit and take these, please. And then I'm calling 911."

Mark was silent as she put her hand on his arm. "Mark, honey, c'mon. Let's get this in you," she pleaded.

His arm fell limp and dangled off the couch.

"Mark?!!"

She put her hand to his forehead. Hot yet clammy. And his skin appeared to have a pale green tint to it. Katie stared at her husband and realized his breathing had stopped. She felt for a pulse; her heart sank when she was unable to find it.

Without hesitation, she positioned herself on top of him and began to perform CPR. How long has it been since his breathing stopped? she thought nervously.

"Mark, damn it, wake up!" Katie said forcefully. "You're not going anywhere on me."

She continued to alternate between the chest compression and the assisted breathing, praying he'd respond. "Mark, please, come back," she implored.

As she moved to apply pressure to his chest once more, his arms twitched. His eyes flew open, but the look in his eyes was bizarre. He appeared to be furious and began to make guttural noises.

"Mark, what is it?"

Her husband lunged at her, threw her off of him and roughly onto the carpet.

"Oh my God!" she yelled. "Mark, stop! Calm down!"

Mark was now sitting up, staring at his hands, seething and shaking. Slowly his bloodshot eyes moved upward, finding hers staring back at him.

"Honey, your heart stopped. I got you back. Now please lay down and let me call the paramedics." Katie began to cry.

And then it happened—she saw it occur. Mark's demeanor went from one of complete rage to a dull expression, except for the hateful glare in his eyes. He stared at her coldly and attempted to stand.

Katie realized this situation was even worse than it had first seemed. Something was tweaked in Mark's head and, whoever this person was across the room from her, he was no longer her husband. At least not now.

Move your ass, she thought. Getting up quickly, she fished in her pocket for her cell phone. Dashing into the kitchen, she grabbed the knife they'd used to slice the pizza. Katie felt absurd doing so, but wasn't taking any chances. She glanced over her shoulder and saw Mark was moving and almost on her. Her mind raced as she screamed and dodged his awkward grab, sending him crashing into the kitchen counter. She ran down the hall to the back bathroom, closed the door, and locked it.

Breathing heavily and trying not to panic, she pulled the cell phone from her pocket and dialed 911. The line rang and rang. Finally a male answered.

"911 operator. What is your emergency?"

Katie hesitated before she spoke, distracted by the high level of chatter she heard behind the operator's voice.

"Hello, are you there?" the operator spoke once more.

"Yes, yes, I'm sorry, I'm here," Katie said in a hushed tone. "My husband fell ill during dinner and I think he may have actually been dead for a moment or two, but he's awake now and angry as hell. I can't get him to talk and he seems to want to hurt me."

"Ma'am, give me your name and address."

"Katie McKinley. We're at 4946 Whipple. Please send someone immediately."

"Hold on. 4946 Whipple. Is that correct, Ms. McKinley?"

"Yes, sir," Katie replied. She could hear banging now in the hallway and a horrible groaning.

"Hold, please," said the operator.

"What? No, I can't hold—" Katie was interrupted by the annoying tones of a mellow guitar on-hold track. "You don't call 911 to be put on hold," she spat to herself.

The groaning in the hallway sounded closer. Every fiber of her being wanted to open the door in order to check on Mark, but she remembered the way he looked at her and knew better. It was up to her to make sure they both got out of this in one piece.

"Okay. ma'am, I'm back. Sorry for the hold," apologized the operator.

"How could you possibly—" Katie began.

"Ma'am, I have to interrupt. Vehicles should be there any moment. It's imperative that you understand me—do not have any further contact with your husband. I can't say this strongly enough: get out of the house *now*!"

With that, the line went dead and she could hear Mark outside the bathroom door. Katie moved to the window by the sink, her fingers shaking as she flipped the little levers to release the screen. Three popped out easily and the last, of course, wouldn't budge. "C'mon," she said out loud. As the doorknob jiggled, she heard the sounds of multiple sirens in the distance. She continued to try to flip the fourth lever. Finally, out of frustration, she took the knife and pried the screen out of the window instead. As it fell inward, a sickening thud fell upon the door and, despite her attempt to stay composed, she screamed.

Katie exhaled and grabbed the crank handle, opening the window slowly. "Turn, damn it," she said and it moved more quickly. Sticking the knife between her teeth, she climbed on top of the sink, braced herself and jumped through the open window. Landing in the grass, she tumbled for a moment, brought herself to her knees, then put the knife back in her hand. From her vantage point, she could see her side lawn and a cross-section of the neighborhood. The world had come unhinged. The colors of emergency vehicles' lights danced on the facades of multiple nearby houses. Down at the Harrington's, smoke was coming from their roof, and over at the O'Donnell's, there appeared to be two bodies on the lawn. What in the world has happened? she wondered.

A loud bang burst from inside the house and a louder growl brought her attention back to the situation. Katie knew Mark could be close behind her and she needed to move. She stood, walked toward the front of the house, and wondered if he'd be able to get through the window, too.

As she came around the corner to the driveway, she froze. No wonder there had been so many flashing lights—there were ten or more emergency vehicles, of varying sizes and types, on her street. The two closest to her home were jet black without markings and looked like no emergency response units she'd ever seen.

Someone tapped Katie's shoulder from behind; she screamed and jumped out of her skin. She whirled around to find three strangers standing behind her, two in what appeared to be hazmat suits and the other pointing a gun at her.

"Katie McKinley?" asked the man in front forcefully.

"I'm K-K-Katie McKinley," she stammered.

Approaching her slowly, he shone the flashlight in her eyes and grabbed her chin, turning her head from side to side, studying her skin. "Katie, I'm Sergeant Metoyer. We've got some kind of outbreak occurring in your neighborhood and I need you to answer two questions for me, please. Have you felt ill tonight and where is your husband?"

"Mark is probably in the bathroom—he's acting completely nuts. There's a window right around the corner," Katie replied nervously, pointing to the side of the house. "And yeah, I felt bad earlier, but I barfed and feel fine now, except for being frightened." She paused. "Is Mark gonna be okay?"

"We don't know yet, but I need you to follow one of these men over to that black truck over there. We're going to verify your condition. Meanwhile, I'm going to attempt to capture your husband without injuring him."

"Please don't hurt him," Katie pleaded.

As one of the hazmat people grabbed her arm and pointed her in the direction of the black truck, Katie saw similar scenarios playing out on the lawns of several homes. She spotted a roadblock at the end of her street and a line of long black bags lying in the street.

Panicking, she turned to look for her husband. "Mark!" she yelled.

Mark came around the corner of the house as if responding to her call. His eyes were ablaze as he snarled and moved in her direction. "Get back!" ordered Metoyer and pulled a taser from his belt, firing at Mark. The voltage dropped Mark to the ground, he flailed and smoldered from the current running through his body. Katie whimpered, straining to reach her spasming husband.

●●●

Later, after Mark had been sedated and restrained with plastic cuffs, he was placed into a breathable body bag and loaded into the back of one of the black vehicles. Katie was told he'd be taken away "for evaluation." She sat on the curb outside a neighbor's home across the street and sipped from a juice box she'd been handed by a paramedic. Metoyer had told her that at least thirteen other situations such as hers had occurred within her neighborhood and the authorities had no idea what the issue was. She was also informed that she could, most likely, see Mark within the next few hours, as soon as the pathogen was identified.

Mrs. Harrington approached Katie and sat next to her on the curb. "I just don't get it," the older woman said. "One minute I'm downstairs doing laundry and Jim's eating pizza and enjoying himself while waiting for the Super Bowl to start. The next thing I know, he's coming after me like a crazy man. If he hadn't been moving so slowly, I could never have outrun him."

Katie stared at her home in the darkness and suddenly lifted her head, reacting to her neighbor's words.

"Hold it. Did you say he was having *pizza*?" Katie asked.

"Yeah, he always orders it for the Super Bowl. Some disgusting combo he likes."

Three miles away, a large black vehicle with a blue flashing light on top sped toward a local lab with fourteen black bags in its cargo area. As the driver turned too quickly into a parking lot, the bags slid hard to one side, knocking them around. Moments later, as if synchronized, the contents of the bags sat up, hissed, and began to tear at the fabric that contained them.

While in town at the Testing Center, consider dining at the nearby

TC'S EPSTEIN BAR & GRILLE —

because

You can do that at TC'S!

Just minutes away from all nine Federal Testing Center locations,
you'll find a TC's Bar & Grille ready and waiting.
Whether it's lunch or dinner, appetizers or simply too many cocktails,
TC's is the place to be before or after the BIG Exam.
Need a steak? How about a steaming slice of Trundle?
Maybe a quiet corner where you can get closer to your escort?

You can do that at TC'S!

Wanna play some slots? Buy gray-market Romerin-2®?
Urinate all over the restrooms?

You can do that at TC'S!

Would you like to be served by a waitress dressed like a cop?
Or be spoon-fed while you stand in a giant crib?

Yup. You can do that at TC'S!

Ask about our Happy Hour Post-Disaster drink specials:
Provo Punch and the Bowl of Shame!
Spend an evening with us and you won't want to go home.

TC'S EPSTEIN BAR & GRILLE —

You can do that at TC'S!

(TC's proudly serves meat from Mack's House of Meats.)

LEADING UP TO THE EXAM, AND ON THE BIG DAY ITSELF

You'd think by now people would know how to behave during an Exam. You'd think wrong. I've seen *so* many people do *so* many inappropriate things over the years that I finally decided to assemble a pre-Exam "Do and Don't List." I guess the Disaster took a bigger psychological toll on us than I thought—it's the only thing that would explain such idiocy.

See if this list helps *you*.

⊙ Several days before your test day, take the sample test in this book (if, by then, you haven't already). Treat the test just like you would the real ZAT by doing everything you'll do on Exam day. The first and most important step: power off your phone. (Do *not* simply switch to vibrate—you need to focus on the test.) And yes, I *did* say "power off your phone"—that

"Thanks for studying with me, Fuzzy, but don't even think about getting a better score than I do unless you'd like to meet Mr. Scissors again."

probably hasn't happened since you got it, right? But, I assure you, the universe will continue to expand. In sum: no talking, no texting, no surfing, no FaceTime, no nothin'! Off it goes.

- ⊙ In addition to neutering your phone, leave the following at home: all type of pods, gaming systems, netbooks, other brands of MP3 players, tablets, streaming media devices of any kind, 3-D goggles, hair dryers, electric toothbrushes and razors, sensory deprivation tanks, and earbuds. Essentially, *any* device that's distracting. I recognize you're not accustomed to doing *anything* without an emo band blasting into your head. Oh well. There *will* be silence in the Testing Chamber.

- ⊙ During the week prior to the Exam, watch as many zombie movies as you can. Indulge in all grades and eras—from the oldest Romero to the staggeringly vapid *Zombiez*. You need to immerse yourself so fully in the genre that, by the time you get to the test, you're oozing minutiae. This approach is certainly no different than studying for the bar exam by watching a *Perry Mason* marathon—it just makes sense.

- ⊙ Don't let anyone talk you out of taking the test. You may not know this, but success can be threatening to those who will never know it. Many people would prefer to see you remain at their level, ordering gizzard baskets and endless pitchers of Pabst. And don't be surprised if many of your supposed friends attempt to deter you from bettering yourself by wanting more from your life than Cheesy Tots (not that there's necessarily anything wrong with Cheesy Tots). Said friends may resort to mocking the very nature of the Ph.Z.

degree and cross-examine you. They might even question its *coolness*, which is pitiable. My advice is tune out those treads. They don't have your best interests at heart. The less you achieve, the more comfortable they are. That's messed up.

⊙ Develop a comfy study routine and stick with it. If you enjoy going to the library, do that. If you're more relaxed in a "gentleman's club," do that. Sitting on a llama in a petting zoo? Whatever. It matters not so much *where* you study, but how *at ease* you are. The point is, find your *special place* and your concentration will be enhanced, on average, by a factor of 3.8.

Remember the adage: "Rest well, test well!"

⊙ The night before, get a good night's rest. Do whatever it takes: melatonin, a pony keg, sleep aids, Blissium®, or a blunt object. By embracing Mr. Sandman, you'll be less likely to nod off during the Exam. The Proctors frown on sleeping and pack brightly colored cattle prods to make their displeasure known.

⊙ Speaking of the night before, do everyone a favor and please lay off all gassy foods. No eggs, no beer, no broccoli, and no bean burritos! You're going to be in an enclosed space with other humans and none of them want to deal with your "farticular" level of stank.

⊙ Many students have started bringing a small Kool Klutch™

"Ew. Who cut one? Did you not read the study guide?"

with them to the Exam so that they have a chilled supply of protein available. You're also welcome to do this, as long you're discreet about it. Note: avoid bringing braunschweiger or other products with a meaty stench.

⊙ As stated, there will only be one limited break period. And even then, the Testing Centers aren't known for their abundant or convenient rest room amenities, and lines form quickly. So consider, as alluded to earlier, wearing a pair of adult diapers. I'm quite fond of the NASA brand, and find them durable and surprisingly sexy. No one wants an accident.

⊙ Keep in mind that there will be a variety of ambitious, degree-hungry people in your testing group and several may be "one fibula short of a leg." Be polite and courteous at all times and there's a strong likelihood no fights will erupt. As a Buddhist friend of mine once said, "Ignore the reed for it is shit."

⊙ No shoes, no shirt—no test for you! Dress appropriately. This isn't your man cave or Lemon-Drop Night with the girls— treat the Exam in a professional manner. Business casual is the proper mode of apparel, as opposed to a Casual Friday look that could involve frightening shorts and Skynyrd-themed tees. And ladies, there's no need to show a lot of cleavage at the Testing Centers. They've seen it all before. Save the knockers for later—we'll talk.

- ⊙ Little-known fact: If you sit in the back and on the right side of the Chamber, statistically you're more likely to get a better grade. The reason for this has yet to be determined, but part of the answer may lie in the fact that the Proctors are less likely to pay attention to you there, which is ideal. Less stress = higher score!

- ⊙ You're encouraged not to interact with your testmates. Granted, there are always a couple of "Chatty Cathies" in every group, but your silence and glowering stares will help convince them to shut the hell up. As stated, this isn't a social event, it's a test.

- ⊙ If you're a smoker, you'll definitely want to wear the "patch" that day. Every Federal Testing Center complex is a smoke-free environment, which is why you'll see crowds of DMV workers and testers puffing away outside in the designated box. Should you attempt to smoke in a restroom or other no-no area, this will be grounds for immediate expulsion and possible flaying.

- ⊙ Lastly, remember to keep an eye on the clock!

I hope these tips were informative and that they will not need to be brought up again. *Comprende?*

• • •

At last we're on the threshold of the Exam itself. After the following commercial message, we'll meet over at the ZAT. Grab a pencil or two and I'll see you there!

INTRO TO THE ZOMBIE EXAM

Warning: you're about to take the Zombie Exam.

(Yes, I *know* it's a sample test, but we want you to start getting a feel for the *real* test and the real test environment, so I'm going to prepare you here for what you'll hear that day as you get ready to start the test.)

This *isn't* the DMV or one of those dopey storefront colleges that tout the urgent need for certified personal trainers. You're in the portion of the complex that's been designated a Federal Testing Center. As far as we can tell, you've shown up here today of your own free will to take this test. If you decide *not* to take the Exam at any point between now and when the starter's pistol is fired, put down

"He claims he lost his nerve at the Testing Center and hasn't felt well since."

your test book and pencil, step away from the desk, and exit the Chamber in a timely and low-key manner. It would probably be best if you keep your back to the door and continually face the Proctors as you exit. That way, no one gets caned. And nobody's going to think less of you for quitting. Much.

By now, we sincerely hope you've done enough research to know the gravity of the task at hand. What you are poised to undertake is akin to, well, nothing you can even imagine. On second thought, consider what it would be like to participate in a Klingon fraternity hazing or be a seasoned jazz musician who gets the call to play on a Justin Bieber session. Either of these situations might approximate what you'll soon endure.

There will be a 20-minute break halfway through the day. Please use that time to "do your duty," have a bite to eat, smoke (only in the designated box in the alley), or what have you. Those students who don't make it back to their seats in time when the pistol is fired again will not be allowed to finish the Exam and will be unceremoniously ushered out of the classroom by the Bouncers. Man, you do *not* want that!

"I don't know about you, Rex, but that Vocabulary section is kicking my arse!"

Remember: read each question and each multiple-choice answer thoroughly before deciding what's correct. *Do not* hand in your Exam until you feel secure about each response or have finally run out of time.

We must say this: thanks for being here. Your love of zombies makes today a special day for us—and we've got your $900 test fee.

Finally, try to enjoy yourself. Though much of the testing process may feel like getting a full Brazilian, I can assure you that, for many, there is much satisfaction to be found in hard work. Personally, I always enjoyed an overstuffed couch.

A man in a striped uniform will soon walk into the room and, at the appointed second, fire his starter's pistol. This will begin the test and signal that you can turn the page. But don't *even* think about it yet. Don't make me call the Bouncers.

Good luck and good testing!

DO NOT PROCEED UNTIL YOU ARE TOLD TO DO SO.
WE'RE LOOKING AT YOU, JIMMY KLEIN!

THE ZOMBIE APTITUDE TEST

(AUTHORIZED SAMPLE)

ETHICS

(Please limit your answers to a paragraph or so—no one's interested in tedious opinions.)

1. As you're driving away from your home, you spot a free-range zombie breaking into your neighbor's house. This is the same neighbor with the constantly barking yippee dogs who sits outside at 11:15 at night and drunkenly bickers with his wife and two older kids who don't have jobs and never says "hello" back when you occasionally make the effort and who keeps a lime-green Gremlin on blocks in the front yard. Do you contact the Paraguard regarding the free-ranger or just call it good? Please explain below.

    ....

    ....

    ....

2. It's your first anniversary with your spouse. After a nice dinner, he/she wants to turn down the lights and watch some geeky show on G4, but you know that *Shaun of the Dead* will be showing on another channel in eighteen minutes. Do you cave in or ask for what *you* want? Please discuss.

3. The National Konstant Keno Program is supposedly designed to boost our lousy economy, but there's evidence to indicate that it's mainly "the poor" who participate, using a portion of their government benefits to play the stupid numbers. Is the Konstant Keno Program doing what it was meant to do or is something else occurring? And why does 40-frickin'-9 *never* come up? Please explain below.

4. A Canadian company that adopted the name "Hal Roach Studios" was responsible for colorizing a number of different classic films, not the least of which was *Night of the Living Dead*. Is it too late to prosecute them to the fullest extent under international laws? Explain how such a thing was ever allowed to happen and why we shouldn't be collectively harassing their descendants.

5. Your President, President Dutch Bingo, is currently in negotiations with a movie production company to lease the National Mall for an

upcoming film shoot that involves zombies. Stressing the size of the country's deficit as his primary reason, Prez Bingo believes the income generated by such a rental is worth the toll the cast and crew may take on our national treasure. (Supposedly, there's a scene toward the end of the film where a number of zombies end up impaled on top of the Washington Monument. That could *rock*.) Furthermore, Bingo would like to use workers from the GAO as living dead extras in the film. If it was up to you, what would you do, and why?

6. Speaking of politics, Senator Frederick Meep has recently proposed closing several facilities in the Scarlet Shores Assisted Post-Living system. His plan involves using the post-lifers contained therein as lettuce pickers in the Sacracisco Valley area. It seems many of the former workers, migrant folks from countries south of the former border, returned to their native lands after the Disaster began. Sen. Meep is claiming that the post-lifers would be more useful to society if deployed in that manner rather than, as he says, "participating in our economy on a leech-like level." Consequently, he's asking for several hundred of the formerly fully living to be used in this capacity. This is becoming a hot topic nationwide. Opposition to his plan is rolling in from large pharma companies and post-human rights groups. Where do you stand? Has a pharma rep offered you free samples yet? Would you be interested in that?

7. The Paraguard has been given a sizeable grant by Code Pinko, a left-wing group, so that the Guard can buy those nifty testing kits that enable one to tell the difference between the recently bitten/post-lifer and a member of the Horde. (You'd think that the violent behavior would be enough but no, apparently, they believe that getting one of the creatures to pee on a plastic stick is the way to go.) The wussies claim that it's inhumane to place a post-lifer in a Containment Zone along with Horde members and, therefore, necessary to know which is which. Sgt. Richard Dick, commander of the Paraguard SouthSouthWestern Brigade, has gone on record as saying "the fleshheads are all the same and I will not endanger one soldier in order to use those damn kits." What the hey is the best way to defuse this situation?

----

8. Within the last few months, scientists have made a startling discovery: zombies actually fear certain vegetables. As improbable as it may sound, it's been observed that Horde members have begun to cower at the sight of cruciferous produce. According to an article published in the *New Jersey Journal of Medicine*, scientists were able to demonstrably alter the behavior of some Horde members by threatening them with bok choy and other garden favorites. What this could mean for battling free-rangers is significant—everyday citizens might be able to fend off an attack by simply waving a cauliflower in a creature's direction. Pentagon researchers are already considering developing a type of "cabbage gas" to augment their arsenals. (Ew.) Can you think of any ethical downside to the militarization of vegetables?

---

9. Chomps, the nearly dead clown enforcer, has been ordered to rough up a corporate guy with whom he used to be friends. He has reservations about this, but knows that his future depends on the fact that he consistently excels at his job. Should Chomps cut the guy a little slack or go ahead and begin the session with the usual sulfuric acid in the Herty-Squirty tie? Explain below.

---

10. Tempe already has a world-class Containment Zone, but a coalition of local businessmen is pushing to build a second one, believing its construction will be good for the community on many levels. Flagstaff could use a facility of its own, what with all those buggers staggering around in the hills by the country club (which galls the golfers). The Flagstaff officials, however, seem to be clueless to the community's needs and, quite honestly, many of those officials continue to hole up in their private fortresses. What solution would serve all parties in the best way? Please explain. And have you thought anymore about one of those great offers from a pharma rep?

11. Upon noticing a free-ranger on their front lawn, Linda and Robert begin discussing their opinions on the zombie issue. Linda feels the living dead are a loutish lot, a drain on society, and wishes they'd just "crawl into the ground and go back where they belong." Robert believes they're misunderstood and wishes more of an effort was made to relate to them. When Linda starts to harp on his stance and tells Robert his position is wimpy, he grabs his rifle from the coat closet, goes outside, and shoots the critter in the head. Coming back inside, he says, "Not so wimpy now, huh? Ya happy?" and slams the door to the den. How could this have played out better? Explain below.

....

....

....

12. The early zombie films featured, almost exclusively, African American actors as zombies. This was most likely due to the "locations" (all

Caribbean, all the time) in the screenplays. In those days, the films had more voodoo, cool drumming, and righteous costumes. Decades later, white folks started catching on to the hipness of the living dead and hijacked the genre from its roots. One could say this is similar to how jazz and later rap were lifted from black culture and placed into potato chip ads and other products that shouldn't require a backbeat. Why do you believe zombie cinema made the leap from the Caribbean to the Hamptons?

....

....

....

13. Horny, the Living Dead Unicorn, has two careers: a spokes-creature for Quali-Ko and a popular motivational speaker on the college campus circuit. Occasionally, given his hectic schedule, Horny has been known to get confused at times and insert endorsements for Quali-Ko into his inspirational speeches. This has caused some controversy. But are his errors really so egregious? I mean, the company *does* foot the travel bill for his speaking engagements. Don't corporations deserve a little love, too? Jeez, they're just people. Anyway, tell us what you think below and you could be eligible to win a free 32 oz. bottle of cool, crisp QualiCola!

....

....

....

14. Jenny's dad moved in with her family several years ago. He was in his late seventies and had a bedroom and his own half bath in the basement. Even though her father was self-sufficient most of the time, Jenny could tell he was starting to lose a little steam.

Unfortunately, his infirmity was accelerated when he was bitten by the UPS guy. Now, Jenny and her husband have to figure out what to do. She believes it wouldn't be in her dad's best interest to put him in a Shores facility. Realistically, there probably isn't an open room. Nevertheless, her husband says that keeping her dad downstairs isn't in *everyone else's* best interest. And he reminds Jenny of two things: all bites are supposed to be reported and the government frowns on people using home care for the bitten. What's the best solution here? And shouldn't UPS make sure their drivers aren't biting innocent people?

15. Scooter recently purchased a Pluggo Jr., the personal version of the Super-Pluggo device. This is the product that fires large blobs of hot glue at a given target, and can come in mighty handy when repairing a security fence or fortifying a basement door. Scooter has been burning through his cartridge supply, while working on his marksmanship. The other day he was caught off-guard by a free-ranger coming up his driveway and, impressing himself, fired a round right onto the creature's head, effectively melting it. This was, of course, fatal to the ranger. Now Scooter's all stoked about his skills and is ready to go full Rambo whenever there's an alert in his neighborhood. What's your take on Scooter's plan?

LOGIC & MATH
(Circle the correct answer.)

1. "Trowel" is to "forehead" as "weed whacker" is to "_____."
   a. shin
   b. gonads
   c. your neighbor's kids
   d. weed?

2. Bob is deader than Shecky. Shecky is less dead than Jimbo. Jimbo is less dead than Skippy. What in the name of Ed Wood does any of this mean?
   a. They're all pretty dead.
   b. Bob is deader than Skippy.
   c. Jimbo is deader than a doornail.
   d. Shecky is only mildly dead.

How's it goin'? Are you keeping an eye on the clock?

3. I'm shambling. If I'm moving at the impressive rate of a block every 9 minutes, but I take 2 minutes off to dine on a passing rabbi, how far will I have traveled after 1 hour 23 minutes?
   a. Kkkkkosher
   b. 9 blocks
   c. A perfectly acceptable distance for somebody like me.
   d. 41 blocks

4. "Incisor" is to "artery " as "Jell-O shot" is to "_____."
   a. breathalyzer
   b. cling peaches
   c. a fine cognac
   d. awesome

5. Jiffy, the post-lifer gone rogue, has a 1-gallon bowl and a 3-gallon bowl. He needs to measure a quart of bread crumbs for a lovely brain loaf he's making. How will he do this?
   a. Fill the 1-gallon bowl only 1/4 of the way. What's so hard?
   b. Are ya kiddin' me? He'll snarf the brain down before he gets it cooked. The guy's an animal.
   c. What a. said, but have the Jiffster put the 3-gallon bowl on his head. He can pull off that look.
   d. I'm not telling Jiffy nothin'. That dude is whack.

6. "Pick-axe" is to "brain stem" as "Ab-Lounge" is to "_____."
   a. flab
   b. ab
   c. stab
   d. Chuck Norris (damn it—that's the *Total Gym*, isn't it?)

7. *Night of the Living Dead* zombies versus *28 Days Later* "zombies." (Yes, we understand there are some issues about whether or not those arc "real" zombies. Humor us.) Who wins?

  a. *28DL* easily. Not even a fair fight.

  b. In a match that went down to the wire, the sheer numbers of *NOTLD* zombies take the *28DL* goofballs in a squeaker!

  c. Hold it—is this logic or math?

  d. It's a draw but I'd like to see what happens when the *NOTLD* zombies get infected by the Rage disease. That'd be killer—like a viral combo platter coursing through their veins.

8. "Branson" is to "art" as "Abba" is to "_____."

  a. Cool Whip

  b. Cadabra

  c. Vegas

  d. Yakov Smirnoff

9. Sociologists have categorized the young people coming of age in these post-Disaster times as "Generation Z." Following this naming convention, what will the next generation be named?

  a. AA

  b. Z2A

  c. A2

  d. What makes you so sure there *will* be another generation?

10. "Provo" is to "pizza" as "Epcot" is to "_____."
   a. travel
   b. Europe
   c. pudding
   d. gondolier

11. Each Liquor Stamp is worth 1/3 of a Garment Stamp. Each Garment Stamp is worth 1/2 of a Cable Stamp. If you'd choose to pay your cable bill one month with Liquor Stamps—which would be a totally stupid idea in my opinion—how many stamps would you owe?
   a. 6
   b. 7 (Don't forget: there's always a 1-stamp penalty for cross-stamp payments.)
   c. 12
   d. 3

12. Lt. Donald "Red" Retch of the C.R.U. claims that in an average month his unit retrieves 114 carcasses. If his unit is one of ten within the district whose averages are all the same, what's the total number of carcasses picked up within that district, for the year?
   a. 13,860
   b. 1,140
   c. 13,680
   d. Um, I think this involves *real* math. You said there wouldn't be equations!

13. Frank owns two InfusoHuts. In a normal month, Hut A does twice the business that Hut B does. Hut A regularly pulls in an amazing 2,400 stamps per month in a crappy location across from a Big Lots.

Lately, though, Hut B has seen a 50 percent increase in its monthly intake, probably because Frank started offering those Happy Hour Hemo-Glowin™ specials. With the most recent numbers crunched, how many stamps per month is Hut B making?

Business is good at INFUSO!

a. 24,000

b. 1,200

c. 1,800

d. 600

14. "Fibula" is to "picnic " as "Auto-Tune" is to "_____."

a. boy bands

b. autos

c. Jiffy Lube

d. Sharonda, your sister's friend, the nail technician who thinks she's the next Beyoncé. Not.

15. "Hoofers & Heavers," a Scarlet Shores Beta dance mixer that meets Thursday nights, has a membership that doubles every week. If they started with 16 members at the end of the first week, what was the membership total at the end of the fourth week?

a. Way too many for that little dance floor. And can they please get a new fog machine? That fog reeks!

b. 128

c. 64

d. 114 (factoring in a reasonable mortality rate)

16. Tragina, the popular avant-garde artist, has painted a series of sitting portraits of Horde members who were apparently heavily tranqued (otherwise I have no idea how they got that weird, 1950s Sears apparel on 'em). Tragina's largest piece, a 10' x 10' effort, which most critics found disturbing, was called the "The Smith Family," and it immediately sold for $16,000. His next largest painting is 7.5' x 7.5' and Tragina claims he will sell it for the proportionate price of the first piece. What will that price be?

a. How did they get that Horde gal's hair in a bouffant?

b. 8,000

c. 12,000

d. I wouldn't give him a dime. I may not know art, but I know what a bunch of deadsacks posing for a Christmas card looks like.

17. "Sharonda" is to "talent" as "corn dog" is to _____.

a. poodle

b. tamale

c. filet mignon

d. Charlie Sheen

18. A national food franchise with ties to the Shores has begun to offer what they call the "Naughty Meal," a boxed selection of pâté, croissants, cheeses, a stick of butter, and an organ meat pie. This meal is obviously targeting zombie fanboy consumers who, surveys show, are interested in eating like their heroes. The franchise's other boxed meal, aimed at children, has 1,200 calories. The Naughty

Meal, on the other hand, purportedly has 9.5 times that amount. If so, how many calories are in a Naughty Meal?

a. An organ meat pie! Where can I get one of those?

b. 11,400

c. 10,800

d. Who cares? Life's shorter than ever—gimme the butter!

19. Oh, that Jiffy—he's trying to cook again. The recipe he's using calls for a cup o' clots, but the only measurement utensil he has is a teaspoon. He vaguely recalls that there are 16 tablespoons in a cup and 3 teaspoons in a tablespoon. How many teaspoons will he need? (And good luck keeping those clots on that little spoon!)

a. 16

b. 32

c. Hold the clots

d. 48

20. "Twinkie" is to "organic" as "Count Chocula" is to "_____."

a. chalk

b. chocolate

c. quinoa

d. Kooky Frooty Puffs

VOCABULARY

(Circle the *most* correct answer.)

1. "Uh, I think Ugar ululates by *undulating* his uvula." In this sentence, *undulating* means _____?

   a. surging

   b. rippling

   c. staggering

   d. rolling

2. "You and I both know that the term 'post-lifer' is simply a *euphemism* for 'mostly dead person.'" In this sentence, *euphemism* means _____?

   a. stand-in

   b. inspiration for

   c. roundabout way of insulting

   d. a nice way of sayin' somethin'

3. "As the fever rose from the infection, the bite mark became bright red and, in turn, Sally became increasingly more *languid*." In this sentence, *languid* means _____?

   a. sexy

   b. flushed

   c. weak

   d. desperate

4. "The *malodorous* fumes coming from the Containment Zone made my wife reach for the oxygen bag." *Malodorous* means _____?

   a. P-U

   b. comical

   c. stinky like a stinky cheese is stinky

   d. tremendous

5. "Hey Pete, patrol says there's a *plethora* of patellas piled up on the parkway." *Plethora* means _____?

   a. gaggle

   b. shit ton

   c. overabundance

   d. gathering

6. "With the help of Romerin-2®, the formerly shy Tammy is now becoming downright *gregarious*." *Gregarious* means _____?

   a. friendly

   b. introverted

   c. outgoing

   d. acting like some guy named "Greg"

7. "After his admittance into Scarlet Shores, Dwayne's demeanor could only be described as *taciturn* at best." In this sentence, *taciturn* means _____?

   a. taking a turn for the worst

   b. uncommunicative

   c. jolly

   d. romantic

"Me? I'm taciturn."

8. "There is *incontrovertible* evidence that the Horde can never be cured so why don't we just off 'em? We could do it as a pay-per-view event and generate some large bank." *Incontrovertible* means _____?

   a. unsubstantiated

   b. unreliable

   c. driving around in your convertible without the top down

   d. undeniable

9. "Despite his advanced behave-mod training, Lenny continued to have a *voracious* appetite every time he got near an attendant." In this sentence, *voracious* means _____?

   a. glamorous

   b. abysmal

   c. bitchin'

   d. ravenous—hungry like the wolf

10. "Cathy acted with such *caprice* when she left so casually for Canada, even her cousins weren't cognizant of her caper." *Caprice* means _____?

   a. malice

   b. fear

   c. Chevy

   d. sudden change of mind

11. "With a decade having passed since the Disaster began, societal bias against the post-lifer population seems relatively *antediluvian*." *Antediluvian* means _____?

    a. a prejudice against the Diluvian empire of the Glatni IV Ringbelt

    b. Is that even English? And who are the Diluvians? Were we invaded and I missed it?

    c. outdated

    d. justified

12. "Fred found that the feeling of fondling a femur was truly *ephemeral*." The word *ephemeral* means _____?

    a. frumpy

    b. folderol

    c. fleeting

    d. for the birds

13. "When the Smith family arrived for Visiting Day, they noticed that Pedro's teeth had a *repugnant* look to them." In this sentence, *repugnant* means _____?

    a. glistening

    b. really, really white

    c. vile

    d. nonexistent

14. "Beaker believes he's found a *taxology* for all Horde members." The word *taxology* means _____?

    a. a way to levy a fee against a group

    b. system of classification

    c. song sung at the end of a spiritual gathering

    d. to stuff or preserve wildlife or pets you like a *whole* lot

15. "Debbie can be particularly *douchey* whenever she dines with Danny." The word *douchey* means _____?

    a. romantic

    b. resembling or having the qualities of a douche

    c. hot

    d. strict

16. "Despite the issues with their son's teeth, the Smith family thought that the Scarlet Shores facility had *assuaged* Pedro's suffering." *Assuaged* means _____?

    a. increased

    b. You said "ass"!

    c. lessened

    d. gotten a kick out of

"Yo."

17. "*Yo*, what the shiz is up?" The word *Yo* means _____?

    a. Well, hello there, old chum!

    b. Uh

    c. Hey

    d. May I have your attention, please?

18. "Harry, the hyper Horde member, is habitually being *harangued* by Hal, the Paraguard guy." In this sentence, *harangued* means _____?

    a. encouraged

    b. being spoken to in an icky way

    c. courted

    d. assaulted

19. "The Smith family was encouraged by their Visiting Day experience with Pedro, except for that deal with his teeth and the fact that his speech was not exactly *perspicuous*." The word *perspicuous* means _____?

    a. audible

    b. in place

    c. a delicious fluid found in the knees

    d. easy to understand

20. "In order to make it through these post-Disaster times, as a society we need a major *paradigm* shift as to how we view ourselves going forward." The word *paradigm* means _____?

    a. 20 cents!

    b. a nickel

    c. archetypical

    d. knee-length

21. "You should take great *solace* from the fact that you've never been bitten and therefore have not had to deal with such horrifying physical symptoms." *Solace* means _____?

a. joy

b. perspective

c. comfort

d. kidney

22. "Sadly, the Smith family's car broke down on the way home. Dad had insisted on taking the very route Google Horde Map had stated was ill-advised, and the entire clan was quickly descended upon. One *auspicious* result of this situation will be that the Smiths will now get to spend *a lot* more time with Pedro." In this case, *auspicious* means _____?

a. cranky

b. stupid

c. favorable

d. sweet

23. "A U.S. president once asked the important question, 'What is *is*?'" In this sentence, *is* means _____?

a. not oral sex

b. is

c. a stain

d. not is

24. "What kind of *besotted* test about zombies has a vocabulary section? This is crunked up." *Besotted* means _____?

   a. dull

   b. hammered like a mofo

   c. dadgum

   d. nebbish-ish

25. "The third one back on the far left—that's the *rapscallion* that abused the Exam with the *besotted* reference. Remove him and, as far as I'm concerned, you don't need to be nice about it." *Rapscallion* means _____?

   a. goner

   b. soon to be screwed

   c. scallywag

   d. exemplary student

26. "It was an innocent question, okay? It just seemed funny to me that you'd have a vocabulary segment in a zombie test. I'll go on back to my desk now. There's absolutely no need to *castigate* me—it won't happen again, I promise." The word *castigate* means _____?

   a. give a stern talking to!

   b. ackkkkkkkkkkkkkkkk!

   c. punish

   d. remove one layer of skin with a vegetable peeler

27. "Although it was *arduous* at first, Abe the Proctor assailed the lad
ad nauseam." *Arduous* means _____?

    a. heartbreaking

    b. scary

    c. difficult

    d. hilarious

CRITICAL READING

(Circle the correct answer.)

1. There's been a great deal of press lately concerning a new trend in
the Scarlet Shores communities and it has some Reggs (uninfected
humans) up in arms—post-lifers having pets. More and more, cats,
dogs and other cuddly critters are showing up in post-lifer residences
and, while apparently comforting to the post-lifer, many Reggs find
this disconcerting. Among their concerns: Are the pets safe, could the
animals somehow become infected, and whose bright idea was this?
Actually, this "inclusion of partner animals" is part of a sociological
pilot program that was initiated by the administrative staff at Omaha's
own Scarlet Shores Beta. In general, the post-lifers make wonderful pet
caretakers and the animals themselves seem to be thriving (though most
are a bit damp from the owners' drooling). The initial data captured
regarding this experiment indicates that, as a result of this warm and
fuzzy addition to their daily post-lives, the post-lifers are needing less
medication, but more Puppy Chow. The long-term effect of this shift
could lead to a need for fewer Drug Stamps and/or the development
of possible Kibble and/or Litter Stamp programs.

a. The writer states that cuddly pets are showing up in post-lifer residences. If that's true, then which of the following might also be a part of the new pet program:
  i. Pythons
  ii. Scorpions
  iii. Bunnies
  iv. Piranhas

b. The phrase "inclusion of partner animals" would best be described as:
  i. Doublespeak
  ii. Eloquent
  iii. Yeah, right—eloquent bullshit is more like it
  iv. The result of too much therapy

c. What's the deal with Reggs?
  i. They're worried they're not getting their fair share.
  ii. They're jealous and always have been. Even when we were kids, they were always whining about what they weren't getting. I used to feel bad for them, but not anymore. Wankers.
  iii. They're simply concerned about the quality of life of the animals that are living with someone who's kinda dead.
  iv. All of the above.

    d. Early results indicate the pets may be having a calming effect on the lifers. If, because of this, fewer Drug Stamps end up being used, then one might believe which of the following could occur:

       i. Liquor Stamp consumption could also dwindle.

       ii. Food Stamp use will increase dramatically.

       iii. Cable Stamp spending will surge.

       iv. Sales of lint rollers will soar.

    e. Based on how the program is going thus far, how would you describe the dynamic:

       i. Post-lifers/Win—Pets/Win.

       ii. Post-lifers/Lose—Pets/Win.

       iii. Reggs are losers *and* whiners.

       iv. It's impossible to tell based on the early data.

2. The first two incarnations of the ZAT were accused of not being racially inclusive. For example, the Critical Reading passages seemed to only reference people with names like "Trent" or "Oliver," with nary a "Juanita" or "TyTeAnna" to be found. Therefore, to balance the scales, here's a story about an ongoing situation in the

Gold is magical!

village of Fishjaw, located in the Northwest Territories of Canada. A year ago, three miles outside of Fishjaw, gold was discovered and subsequently, the town has experienced a bona fide gold rush. The rush has filled this tiny town with all manner of interesting people such as Agnostic Filipinos, Jewish-Chinese workers, a contingent of African Americans with hot Latina girlfriends, and, as always, the cross-dressing Eskimos. As it turns out, a goodly number of the citizens of Fishjaw are not comfortable with the influx of diversity. Fortunately, the townsfolk are an unusually repressed group and have been nothing but polite to the newcomers. All in all, the gold rush has brought a much-needed economic shot in the arm to Fishjaw and has taught everyone that it *is* possible for human beings from diverse backgrounds to get along if there's enough money to be made. Wasn't that a nice story? The ZAT's come a long way.

a. Which statement below accurately reflects why this passage was a part of this Exam?

   i. People of color should be hired to write more textbooks and exams.

   ii. White people have stuck-up names.

   iii. Fishjaw needs the press.

   iv. This was a completely gratuitous attempt to give the impression that the Exam has become racially inclusive, Trent.

b. When it comes to gold, how would you say it impacts a community?

   i. Gold has magical properties that bring people together.

   ii. Gold encourages the best behavior in everyone.

   iii. Gold is a divider of men, while silver plays nicely with others.

   iv. Now platinum—that's a pip of a metal!

c. Concerning the people of Fishjaw, which is the most accurate statement regarding their collective character?

  i. A bunch of two-faced hicks who probably built their town on land they stole from the Inuits.

  ii. Well-meaning folks who are struggling to embrace an invasion of strangers to their village, especially those cross-dressers.

  iii. A typical group of humans, brimming with either compassion or disgust toward those they don't understand.

  iv. A lot like those lovable characters on *Northern Exposure*—quirky and carefree, but with far fewer teeth.

d. "Agnostic Filipinos, Jewish Chinese workers, a contingent of African Americans with hot Latina girlfriends, and, as always, the cross-dressing Eskimos." In your opinion, what does this collection indicate about the nature of our modern world?

  i. We're confused.

  ii. As races and religions continue to commingle, we're becoming a blended world where, one day, we'll be one big pink/yellow/brown hybrid worshipping God in whatever way we choose, while still despising those who don't agree with us.

  iii. Latinas are smokin'!

  iv. Canada is no longer the last frontier for white guys.

3. Omaha's own Scarlet Shores Beta has once again created a cutting-edge advancement in living concepts. That sassy facility has introduced what's called "franchise nesting." Here's how it works: in their enormous Betatrium, a new Subway sandwich store has been installed. Inside that fine restaurant, a local bank has opened a full-service mini-branch with one teller and an ATM (which, of course, only dispenses stamps) and, inside that branch, a savvy group opened a Starbucks! The efficiency of the nesting model can't be denied and, according to Benjamin Cheeks, Chief Franchising Officer of Shores, LLC, this could be the future of franchise expansion within the national Shores system. "The interesting part is, whatever products the residents were attracted to in their former lives, they continue to be attracted to now. Our research shows a big post-lifer thumb up—spending has increased and croaking is down." Cheeks says he can envision a number of other useful amalgamations of familiar or comforting brands such as nested Burger Kings, Walgreens, and Panda Inns.

   a. Regarding this new nesting business plan, what might be a few of the ethical issues here? Circle the answer below that should *not* to be considered.

      i.   Undue influence exerted by corporate yokels who are buying their way into a literal captive audience.

      ii. Repeated coffee stains on the lone bank teller.

      iii. Frighteningly cheerful and loud Starbucks baristas will annoy the other five employees in "the nest."

      iv. Due to the superior shopping environment, more civilians will come to visit their post-lifer relatives. Strain on system?

b. According to this passage, Scarlet Shores Beta thinks pretty highly of itself and can seem stuck-up at times. Is there an answer below that explains why its lofty opinion of itself may be accurate?

    i. The presence of a round-the-clock Pork 'n' Pill Bar in the Betatrium.

    ii. The biggest and cleanest QCasino in the whole system, baby!

    iii. "Bottomless Brains Night" Tuesdays in the Hall o' Fixins.

    iv. All of the above.

c. Below are five different nesting combos. Circle the one you like the best.

    i. Cold Stone Creamery, Bank of America, Smart Car Dealership

    ii. Long John Silvers, Christian Science Reading Room, Blinky's Mad Tatts

    iii. In-N-Out Burger, Verizon, Uncle Skippy's Adult Novelties

    iv. Chipotle, Wells Fargo, The Taxidermy Shed

d. The term "advancement in living concepts" most likely means what here?

    i. A more efficient and profitable use of resources.

    ii. Why would the word "living" even be used?

    iii. Sorry, I'm still stuck on the other question. I haven't even heard of a place called "Uncle Skippy's Adult Novelties." Is that an appropriate name for a dildo store?

    iv. Usually a euphemism (see *Vocabulary* segment) for actions that lead to downgrades in services and a reduced number of healthy options.

4. In the most recent elections, the Post-Lifer Party lost control of Congress by a strong push from the Horde Party. A record turnout by voters (nearly 23 percent!) indicated that there was a strong dissatisfaction with both main parties, but many felt that the Post-Lifer Party had done the worst job by not solving the country's problems within months. Instead, voters turned to the new kid on the block, the Cranial Party, which believes the other two parties are corrupt, but sucked up to the Horde Party to get the most press and promotional swag. Outgoing Majority Leader Debi Accckkkkfff said she was "disappointed in the results, but we'll stagger back to the capital and return to work." The Cranial Party is working on finding a candidate who has all his teeth in order to get him or her onto the presidential ticket in two years. Many in the know believe that Gland Peters appears to be the front-runner for the Cranials, if he can rein in the flatulence. The Horde Party has already begun to distance itself from several of the more "conservatively radical" positions of the Cranials, such as mandatory handguns for all citizens, a proposed tax on the government's Cable Stamp program, and "Triple-Bacon Wednesdays" at all federal cafeterias. If you like politics (and who doesn't?), the next couple of years look like they'll be more intriguing than ever.

a. Regarding the aforementioned election results, which statement would be most accurate?

   i. Voters are so annoyed with both "lamestream" parties that they're willing to elect toothless maverick nincompoops.

   ii. The Post-Lifer Party is kaput.

   iii. The Horde Party made gains, but the Cranials took terrain that fell mainly on the plains.

   iv. It's all a bunch of crap because there is no real government, merely puppets performing as directed. And QualiCorps has their hands up the butt of every one of 'em. If you believe anything other than that, you're fooling yourself.

b. Why would the Cranial Party align itself with the Horde Party at all?

   i. The Horde Party had most of the momentum going into the election and the Cranial Party wanted in on that action.

   ii. The Cranial Party's core values more closely resemble those of the Horde's, especially their "No-Life" stance.

   iii. The Horde Party has members who are downright dreamy.

   iv. Who knows, but next time I'm votin' Whig!

c. In this story, what does the term "conservatively radical" mean?

   i. Like Republicans, but way more rad

   ii. It's the opposite of "liberally superficial."

   iii. A political stance somewhere between Mussolini and Fred Durst

   iv. Jacksquat

    d. What kind of last name is "Accckkkkfff?"

       i. Pennsylvania Dutch?

      ii. It's one of those, you know, "honor names" some folks are adopting to support the post-lifers. They rename themselves to stand (more like "slump") in solidarity with the fleshheads.

    iii. Definitely British.

    iv. I had an Aunt Sally whose last name was Acckkff. I wonder if I'm somehow related to the outgoing Majority Leader?

5. With the tremendous response from applicants hoping to take the ZAT, the Capon Académie is starting to see a sizeable financial windfall. The school's administration would like to take that money and improve the facilities by adding two wings to the existing main building. The Bored of Regents, on the other hand, has a vision of franchising the school and taking it stateside. Their idea

Here, the Académie's own Chancellor van Dyne poses with a bag of money.

is to develop the Académie "brand" and place educational outlets in every remaining state. They've also spoken about a series of coffee shops opening under the "Capon Coffee" name. However, most Regents believe that associating a castrated rooster with a beverage won't be appealing. Meanwhile, the Gaggle of Governors is strongly advising the Académie to hold onto its money until it's been determined whether the ZAT is a certified hit or a brief moronic fad. The three sides are currently at an impasse and, if the situation doesn't improve, a mediator may have to be brought in to break up the occasional fisticuffs.

a. Choose the most reasonable solution to the impasse from the choices below.

   i. Go stateside—all in, baby!

   ii. Keep it as it is; don't let Chancellor van Dyne anywhere near the cash.

   iii. Think bigger—offer an IPO!

   iv. Governors assemble in a "gaggle?" Huh.

b. Why a castrated rooster?

   i. Dames dig it.

   ii. Seems less threatening than a big ol' rooster waving his unit around like a magic wand.

   iii. Well, they're popular in certain rituals and the meat is more tender than your standard rooster.

   iv. He makes for an entertaining mascot—it's funny because he has a giant Band-Aid on his butt!

    c. "Brief moronic fad" feels meanspirited, but how could such a thing happen?

        i. The collective attention span of our society is akin to a moth—consumers find a bright new object, flock to it, and then don't.

        ii. Graduates discover the degree doesn't have the same impact on their lives as they believed it would. Shocker.

        iii. A vampire school opens nearby and kicks the Académie's ass.

        iv. It's just change, man. It happens.

6. It appeared that Terry had painted himself into a corner, as it were, trapped in his neighbor's basement. He'd stopped by because he'd heard unusual sounds coming from the home of Kitty, his elderly neighbor. Terry knocked on her door but there wasn't a response. Finding the door ajar, he let himself in and, while exploring, discovered the place had a half dozen living dead roaming around, including Kitty herself. When Terry attempted to leave the way he came, two zombies were blocking his path. *Why didn't I pack a gun?* he thought. Next, he rushed down the hallway and was confronted by another staggering fleshhead, this one missing his left arm. Without thinking, Terry grabbed the nearest doorknob, went inside, and locked the door behind him. He was initially relieved to find himself in the basement. As he descended the stairs, he realized he'd made the wrong choice: Kitty had a walkout basement with an array of floor-to-ceiling windows. As a result, Terry was in the equivalent of a display case. Unfortunately, dozens of living dead had spilled over into Kitty's backyard and had noticed Terry. "Damn—I'm a lobster in a lobster tank," he muttered.

a. If you knock on a neighbor's door and there's no answer, do *you* let yourself in? Why or why not?

    i. Heaven's no. Especially if it's that Kitty woman, with her flimsy nighties and half-open robes!

    ii. Sure, I let myself into all sorts of people's homes. I try on their clothes, feed their pets, and maybe make a sandwich or two. It's neighborly!

    iii. I don't think so. Kitty has been known to have "gentleman callers" and I don't wanna witness that.

    iv. Probably not. The other day I stopped to help a person with a car problem and almost got bitten by an infected biker cop. The best thing a Good Samaritan can do is stay alive!

b. In the story, we have no idea how Kitty got infected. What's the deal there?

    i. The writer can't monitor everything that's going on—cut him some slack.

    ii. Lazy prose.

    iii. It's not relevant to the rest of the scene.

    iv. Maybe Terry bit her. That'd be a twist, huh?

c. If you were Terry, what would you do?

    i. See if there's an egress window anywhere in the basement and try to escape.

    ii. Take the fireplace poker from the basement hearth and make a run for it.

    iii. Think. Didn't Kitty used to talk about having a panic room? It must be in the basement!

    iv. Try the door that leads to the garage. Maybe her keys are in the ignition and you can back out and take down a few of those shambling fools.

7. Dr. Lance Boyle, Chief Behavioral Technician for Scarlet Shores, Inc., has introduced "operant conditioning" to post-lifers. This low-grade training, it is hoped, will help the lifers to more quickly obey commands and help them better adapt to their responsibilities under the newly deployed Share Care System™. Through the use of a clicker and a positive reinforcement reward—such as a meatball upon completion of a task—post-lifers can be trained to get

Mrs. Dr. Lance Boyle says: "The Share Care System works for everyone!"

themselves to an appointed pill station at the correct time. Using this conditioning to move residents from points A to B will boost efficiency for all concerned. Sadly, this could eventually lead to downsizing the staff, but on the bright side that could save money in the long run. Dr. Boyle says, "We believe operant conditioning will assist us in fully implementing our Share Care System, which will lead to a healthier and streamlined client environment." Boyle, a former lemur trainer at the Henry Doorly Zoo in Omaha, has won multiple awards for his work in behavior modification and was the first scientist to advocate the use of cocktail franks as reinforcement rewards for his arboreal former clients (even though they are usually herbivores). We'll want to check back with Dr. Boyle to get a feel for the Share Care System's effectiveness on a national scale.

a. Once Dr. Boyle's program is rolled out at every Shores, there may be certain side effects. Select the most likely effects below.

   i.   Fewer workers are needed, layoffs are justified, post-lifers are more consistently dosed and don't notice the lack of staff. The Shores nearly run themselves!

   ii. Apathy and weight gain.

   iii. Stocks of companies that produce meatballs and cocktail franks soar.

   iv. Let me get this straight—under the Share Care System, you have patients assuming responsibility for part of their own recovery? Wow—that's either brilliant or incredibly evil. Don't let United Health Care find out about this.

b. Harkening back to the Share Care System for a moment (and keeping an open mind, please), why might it be an acceptable idea for clients to begin "pitching in" a little? Their government stamp supply is nearly bottomless and their care and feeding would certainly be considered more than adequate. The remaining citizens of this country have made great sacrifices on their behalf. Your take?

   i.   Well, when you put it like that, I guess there isn't anything wrong with simply asking them to walk from their apartments over to a pill station. I mean, what lazy bastards!

   ii. It's *wrong*. Healing cannot be forced on a timetable. Post-lifers are part of our extended family and deserve better. Making the conditioning voluntary is one thing, but mandatory training isn't right.

   iii. Get the damn fleshheads to take their sorry asses over to the pill station and, while they're at it, have them wax the cafeteria floor or vacuum the rug in the QCasino. Or let 'em go pick lettuce, I don't care but, for Pete's sake, make 'em work for a post-living!

   iv. We're never going to find a cure. Pair 'em up with the Horde and be done with it.

c. In this passage, we're informed of a former lemur trainer being given a position where he's in charge of modifying behaviors within what can only be considered the equivalent of a chain of retirement homes. How can that be right?

   i. Lemurs are primates, but not quite dues-paying monkeys (belonging to the *prosimian* group, which, by the way, is *not* a group that holds pro-simian rallies). Similarly, post-lifers are related to primates, but not quite human. By establishing this distant genetic connection, it becomes easier to know what will work within a "behave-mod" environment. In other words, Boyle had rep.

   ii. Number i., above, is full of shit.

   iii. Experts are in short supply in these post-Disaster times. Hell, any dweeb with a toolbox can be a plane mechanic nowadays and that seems way more wrong to me. I say, let's see what our good monkey advocate can do!

   iv. I've got a cousin in the Tucson Scarlet Shores. He actually smiled at me the other day when we were doing the allotted Video Family Time. Let me tell you, getting a smile out of him is huge progress. At every other VFT event, he only lunged at the webcam. If this change in behavior is because of Boyle, then let him keep doing whatever he's doing. I think it might be working.

8. Your President, President Dutch Bingo, has come out firmly in favor of a proposal by the Cranial Party. The idea being bandied about is one that mandates the cessation of new Containment Zone construction and, instead, suggests that we wall off the eastern third of Montana and place Horde members there. The long-term goal is to have the entire Horde in one location. Over time, if the situation allowed, older Zones would be closed and Horde members would be sleep-gassed and transferred to the new locale. The savings to taxpayers would be enormous. Prez Bingo has also made it clear that he would prefer to see a shift in our citizenry's belief that Horde members need to be preserved like the post-lifers. His recent statement regarding this was: "Hey man, those *just* aren't your relatives anymore—get over it." Meanwhile, the folks in eastern Montana aren't so fond of this idea and believe Utah should have to bear the brunt of whatever Horde solution is ultimately adopted because of Utah's almost-parental relationship with the virus. More than likely, a vote will come to the floor of Congress next summer and, with any luck, could become law within 9 to 12 years.

a. According to the Cranial Party proposal, it would appear that the construction costs of walling off part of Montana would be offset by the savings accrued from ending the construction of Containment Zones. Additionally, the presence of Paraguard troops would eventually shift from the Zones

"Tick, tick, tick..."

to the protection of local areas. What's the most likely outcome of this approach?

    i. Montana rakes in government support and *big* tourist dollars!

    ii. The Paraguard is absorbed into local law enforcement agencies, and donut shops thrive.

    iii. Montana declares war on Utah and I, for one, can't wait to see how that shakes out! Throwdown grandé!

    iv. Lemme guess—everything continues to go to hell?

b. While not discussed here, which selection below best explains the evolution of the Cranial Party:

    i. Disgruntled C.R.U. officials form new political party based on trying to curtail the monies spent on helping the living dead.

    ii. One faction of the Tea Party becomes the Cocoa Party, splinters into the Cookie Party, which then morphs into the People's Party, and settles on the ironic name of the Cranial Party and orders cute hats.

    iii. Millions of years ago, a small mammal crawls from the mud. A few months pass and—*POOF*—he magically becomes a chimp. A decade later, he's a feller and has hooked up with a hominid chick. Cranial Party follows shortly thereafter.

    iv. A Libertarian mated with a Marxist.

c. Regarding Bingo's position about the Horde and how the creatures are no longer anyone's relatives, what would be the benefits to society if he got his wish?

i. More money for the living—hey, that would be nice.

ii. While we're at it, maybe it's time to look at the "status" of the post-lifers, too. They sure soak up a lot of stamps and space.

iii. No eastern Montana veldt, no Containment Zones. Gas 'em and be done with it. Clean slate, baby.

iv. Open the zones as "Hunting Compounds" and charge a hefty admission price.

GEOGRAPHY, HISTORY, & THE SOCIAL SCIENCES

(Circle the correct answer.)

1. Haiti shares the island of Hispaniola (a name that I thought was one of Prince's sexy protégées) with what other country?
   a. Spain
   b. The Dominican Republic
   c. You do realize Spain is not part of an island, right?
   d. Kluckistan

2. What famous nature painter was born in Les Ceyes in 1785?
   a. Why is that relevant?
   b. Miro
   c. It's part of the history of the area where zombies originated and it's important that you know some of this stuff or I wouldn't be asking you. You can expect a cameo appearance from a Proctor soon.
   d. John James Audubon

3. In 1492, Christopher Columbus landed on the shores of Hispaniola, promptly claiming the island for Spain. Can anyone give me a good explanation why this fascist turd deserves a holiday named after him?
   a. No, I can't. He treated the natives badly and deserves nada.
   b. So he wasn't a saint—he still accomplished amazing things in his era. He helped discover America, after all.
   c. Well, actually that's not true about him discovering America. Many historians now believe that, in 1421, a Chinese admiral named Ho had first dibs on the continent. I say the holiday should be renamed "Ho-Day." Has a nice ring to it, eh?

d. Talk about off-point. Columbus was a multifaceted character—a remarkable explorer but also a schmuck who kidnapped natives and took them back to Spain to show 'em off. Lame.

4. In governmental studies, "average zombie" (aka, member of the Horde) is a formal term. Choose the correct definition below.

a. 5-foot 9-inch 28-year-old white male, wearing a T-shirt that references an obscure metal band, of portly build with Cheeto stains still on his fingers.

b. 5-foot 5-inch 33-year-old black female, McHottie with a bitchin' weave and slammin' stilettos.

c. 6-foot 32-year-old male of mixed race, former assistant manager of a Hooters who fancies himself to be the next MMA star and does a mean Marvin Gaye in the shower.

d. 5-foot 8-inch 62-year-old white male, still in a cardigan, found outside of his home, waiting at the mailbox for his wiener pills to arrive.

5. The drug Productiva® has been scientifically proven to motivate post-lifers to such a degree that they're now capable of leading an "active" lifestyle (and, boy oh boy, do we ever mean those quotes). What were the original uses for the drug?

a. Antidepressant and canine diet pill.

b. Pro-depressant and cattle fattener.

c. Hyperactivity aid and diuretic.

d. Impotence relief and mega-metabolism booster.

6. The zomfather, Mr. Romero, shot *Night of the Living Dead* in which state?

    a. New Jersey

    b. Alabama

    c. Pennsylvania

    d. At a posh resort in upstate Vermont with the cutest little cabin-shaped maple syrup bottles for sale in the gift shop.

7. One more Columbus question: that prick left part of his crew behind to settle Hispaniola in 1492, but when he came back a year later, they were gone. What happened?

    a. The villagers ate 'em.

    b. Those folks amscrayed into the unglejay. They didn't ever want to deal with Columbus again.

    c. It's obvious—they became zombies.

    d. They married into the villagers' clans and then took up with their native kin, like in *Dances with Wolves*. But this was way different 'cause there were no wolves or Costners. Or dances.

8. In America, voodoo practice flourished for years in what state?

    a. Brooklyn?

    b. Minnesota?

    c. The power was most strong in Louisiana.

    d. I'm pretty sure it was West Virginia. Them mines make nice sites for rituals.

9. The snake was a popular symbol in voodoo ceremonies and was known as what?

   a. The Astonishing Slither-Man

   b. Juan

   c. Li Grand Zombi

   d. Snakey, the wonder serpent

Early zombie settlers head north to a mythical land called Oklahoma.

10. Research tells us that, in major urban areas, quite frequently the living dead "of color" outnumber the white living dead by 3 to 1. Why would that be?

   a. Because all the whiteys moved to the suburbs and bought their giant houses, leaving the inner cities to crumble without the whitey tax base. I tell you what, though—zombies like them some malls and the whiteys do, too, and that's where the karmic justice will go down, my brothuh. Know what I'm sayin'?

   b. Densely populated vertical housing is usually inhabited by minorities. An urban outbreak is therefore going to be more racially lopsided.

   c. When the shit goes down, white people can afford a cab to get out of Dodge.

   d. Ain't that a bitch? We *finally* get ourselves into a majority and it involves the living dead.

11. For the most part, the outbreak appears to have stopped spreading in Canada. What is the current theory regarding why?

a. The virus is sorta like the Blob—it doesn't like the cold and is a bit of a "snowbird," choosing to winter in Yuma.

b. The virus thinks the world of Neil Young's body of work. And it swears it must've worn out three copies of the vinyl version of Joni Mitchell's *Blue*.

c. Canadian dollar conversion rate is too daunting for the virus.

d. Despite being mostly dead, many zombies continue to have a fine sense of fashion and are repulsed by plaid.

12. That screwy movie *C.H.U.D.*—its quasi-zombies lurked where?

    a. In your closet, waiting for you to fall asleep.

    b. Underneath a Super Target in Wichita.

    c. In the sewers of New York.

    d. Inside the dressing rooms at H&M.

13. In 1697, the Treaty of Ryswick divided Hispaniola into two parts. Who controlled the two sections?

    a. Spain and a different Spain, which was smaller than the real Spain and was continually sued for calling itself "Spain"

    b. Kluckistan and Bulgaria

    c. France and Spain

    d. France and Fredonia

14. In voodoo practices, a family spirit is called what?

    a. Trixie

    b. Bob

    c. Loua

    d. Louie

15. The highest point is Haiti is what?

    a. Every Friday night at the Limpin' Dubliner, which is the revolving Irish pub at the top of QualiCorps Tower in downtown Port-au-Prince

    b. Mt. Charo

    c. Chain de la Selle

    d. Atop the "Papa Doc," that enormous Ferris wheel at Paradise Park

MEAT

(Circle the most delicious answer.)

1. "Sweetbreads" are actually what part of a body?
    a. Lips
    b. Lymph nodes
    c. Biscuits
    d. Thymus gland and/or pancreas

2. Contrary to the eating habits of the contained Horde, a free-ranger will, 90 percent of the time, initially lunge for what human body part?
    a. Arms
    b. Femur
    c. Crotchal region
    d. Skull

3. Catholic post-lifers are annoyed every year when Lent rolls around due to the "fish on Fridays" issue. What have the amazing folks at QualiCorps Labs come up with to ease the lifers' misery?
    a. Trundle Sticks
    b. Catfish bred with the bacon gene
    c. Cows with gills
    d. Otter Burgers

4. Speaking of bacon, it's common knowledge that it is now considered to be a "superfood," akin to blueberries and pomegranates. In days of old, unenlightened folks (including scientists) believed otherwise. Name the property below that is *not* a beneficial effect of consuming bacon:

a. It's a powerful aphrodisiac.

b. It's rich in antioxidants.

c. The grease is packed with oils essential to the proper well-being of hair, fingernails, and cheeseburgers.

d. A triple bypass.

5. Marrow is something you really shouldn't let anyone suck out of you. Why?

a. It part of bone and bone good.

b. You need it to live, doof.

c. You'd have to be pretty dead to let someone do that.

When dining out, always ask for meat from Mack's. Whether it's Trundle or just a slice of LoafLike, you can get it at Mack's. C'mon over to our house—Mack's House of Meats.

d. Marrow-sucking should not occur before the third date.

6. Two popular prehistoric singers, Doris Day and Frankie Laine, recorded a song called "How Lovely Cooks the _____."

a. Goose

b. Green Bean Casserole with Those Little Crispy Onions on Top

c. Scrapple

d. Meat

7. "Marbling" in meat refers to what?

   a. I'm vegan, remember? Get some sensitivity training.

   b. The yummy fat within muscles.

   c. Wrapping the meat in other meat and then in an Ace Bandage, soaking it in brine for 72 hours, and then hanging it in a warm, humid room for a week.

   d. A particular way of slicing meat for maximum tenderness.

8. Some Containment Zones have begun using what as a protein source for the Horde?

   a. Smart Dogs

   b. LoafLike

   c. Egg salad

   d. Mac and cheese

9. A certain fast-food chain caught hell when the ingredients in their "taco meat filling" were revealed. Name the ingredient that was *not* on the macabre list.

   a. Isolated Oat Product

   b. Beef

   c. Autolyzed Yeast Extract

   d. Meat Dye #9

10. Some fella at a Michigan institute of supposedly higher learning has surmised that ancient man was able to preserve his meat for months by using what?

    a. Kro-Magnon Kool Klutch™

    b. The Kenmore Hollowed-Out Wooly Mammoth Deluxe

    c. His pants

    d. A frozen lake

11. The poet Robert Burns once wrote about a meat dish: "The groaning platter there you fill, your buttocks like a distant hill" in a poem called "Address to a _____." (And Burns, get a better topic next time, willya?)

    a. Kabob

    b. Chalupa

    c. Haggis

    d. Cheddarwurst

12. Given a choice, zombies prefer what food source to dining on humans?

    a. Horse—it's like a freakin' delicacy to them.

    b. Burgers—even when humans are dead, they still love 'em!

    c. Sparrow—not very meaty but you can eat, like, 40 or 50.

    d. Chimichangas—grease is still the word.

13. Back when cows were more plentiful, a 1,000-lb. steer would provide how much meat?

   a. 902 lbs.

   b. 540 lbs.

   c. 430 lbs.

   d. Just enough

14. Speaking of our bovine friends, the first cattle were brought to the Western Hemisphere by whom?

   a. That creep Columbus

   b. That goofy Magellan

   c. The playuh known as B-Frank, Mr. Franklin if you're nasty

   d. Those blasted pilgrims

15. Another holiday that used to be celebrated was *the* day of the year for beef consumption. That holiday was?

   a. Red Meat Day—it's the third Tuesday in August

   b. The Annual Block Party at Hollywood and Bovine

   c. CowFest—traditionally begun eleven days after Dyngus Day, which is always the Monday after Easter

   d. Memorial Day

16. This question is "anti-meat" related. As stated earlier, scientists have recently discovered that zombies are repulsed by veggies. Which vegetable seems to work the best?

   a. Ketchup

   b. Broccoli

   c. My Uncle Lew

   d. Brussels sprouts

17. Back when pigs were plentiful, they were occasionally used on battlefields as what?

   a. Truffle detectors

   b. Dinner

   c. Mine sniffers

   d. Adorable, delectable decoys

18. The singer Meat Loaf has had how many concussions?

   a. 2

   b. 8

   c. 17

   d. huh?

19. Who knew meat could be so patriotic? What country has a "national chicken"?

   a. Canada

   b. Switzerland

   c. South Korea

   d. Kluckistan

ZOMBIE LORE & MOVIE TRIVIA
(Circle the correct answer.)

1. The budget for George Romero's 1968 *Night of the Living Dead* was:
   a. $12,000.00
   b. An arm and a leg (zing!)
   c. Lots
   d. $114,000.00

2. Okay, smarty-pants—the original title of *Night of the Living Dead* was:
   a. *Night of the Motor-Skills Challenged*
   b. *Weekend at Bernie's*
   c. *Night of the Flesh Eaters*
   d. *Road House*

3. According to voodoo legend, if you'd like a zombie to return to the grave, feed it this (and while you're feeding it, put a bib on it too—they're *sooo* messy):
   a. Salt
   b. Tartar sauce
   c. Oysters
   d. An Altoid

4. *Invisible Invaders* from 1958 featured a number of nattily dressed
   reanimated dead. Who was inhabiting the corpses?
   a. Squatters
   b. Stoners from another dimension
   c. Aliens who'd lived on the moon for 20,000 years!
   d. A group bent on destroying our Constitution

5. Zombies are thought to be named after "Zombi," the voodoo god of:
   a. Side-by-side refrigerators
   b. Inflatable furniture
   c. Snakes
   d. Wham-O products

6. Name the tagline from *Zombie*, the Italian classic from 1979:

   a. "Nice to meat you."

   b. "We are going to scare you now, I tell you what."

   c. "Mangia, mangia!"

   d. "We are going to eat you."

7. That giant zombie dude in *Plan 9 from Outer Space*—what was his name?

   a. Andre the giant zombie dude

   b. Adrian Brody

   c. Tor Johnson

   d. Adam West

8. In *Shaun of the Dead*, name Shaun's favorite zombie-killing weapon?

   a. Meat thermometer

   b. Trowel

   c. Margaret Thatcher

   d. Cricket bat

9. The soundtrack to Dan O'Bannon's 1985 film, *Return of the Living Dead* (who knew they were missing?), became a cult hit by featuring a number of perky deathrock tunes. Which one of these songs was *not* in the soundtrack?

   a. *Tonight (We'll Make Love Until We Die)*

   b. *Eyes Without a Face*

   c. *Margaret Thatcher*

   d. *Surfin' Dead*

10. What are lwa?

   a. Choking sounds one makes right before the Heimlich is applied.

   b. The question should be "what *is* the LWA." It's the Lifeless Workers of America organization, a group that's trying to unionize post-lifers.

   c. Spirits in voodoo religion.

   d. Tiny sippy cups used for the drinking of potions.

11. Ray Dennis Steckler was a legendary (well, I may be stretching the definition a bit) "B" movie director. He was most well-known for the classic, *The Incredibly Strange Creatures Who Stopped Living and Became Mixed-Up Zombies*. It takes a special kind of filmmaker to assemble the body of work he had. Which of the movies below is *not* one of his?

   a. *The Sexorcist*

   b. *Rat Pfink a Boo Boo*

   c. *The Mad Love Life of a Hot Vampire*

   d. *Gone with the Wendigo*

12. Wayyyyy back in 1984, the very first zombie video game was released in Britain. It was called what?

   a. Bytes and Bites—The Trials of Jack Zombiekiller

   b. Zombie Zombie

   c. Ms. Pac Dead Man

   d. Killshot, the Man Who Never Misses

"It won't be long now."

13. "The *Halloween* series of films are zombie-related by their very nature because Michael Myers is, essentially, a living dead entity." Which answer below would you say best proves or negates this statement?

a. No way. Michael is more supernatural and apparently can't be killed, but that has diddly to do with zombies, so I'm gonna have to say "false."

b. Lay off the ganja, bruh. He's supposedly dead and he returns to life. And Rob *Zombie* even directed a remake. Do you need more proof than that? But what's with that mask—zombies don't need masks! Anyway, he's got my vote.

c. You're both damaged goods. He was never infected so how in the world could he be a zombie? He's more like a werewolf or a Chupacabra—a mystical maniac. So no, he's not a zombie, but he's certainly got a degree of awesomeness to him. And the films usually feature lovely breasts.

d. Zero for three, lads. The truth is he's a hybrid—several things simultaneously. He *is* a zombie because he's dead and moving rather well for a guy in his condition. At the same time, he's *also* a myth and a force of nature who's always up for a sequel. He's a man, he's a monster, but what I bet you *don't* know is he may be a killing machine, but he has a weakness for bunnies. No kidding. He's a breeder. He even shows them and has won a bunch of blue ribbons.

14. Bela Lugosi, usually known for his vampire antics, starred in a 1932 film that's regarded as the first zombie movie. What was it called?

    a. *Two Shambling Guys*

    b. *White Zombie*

    c. *Beige Zombie*

    d. *Mauve Zombie*

15. In the aforementioned film, Mr. Lugosi had a power he used on his zombie sugar-mill employees. What was that power?

    a. Meat vision

    b. Stupor-hearing

    c. Hypnotic gaze/mind control

    d. Incredible minty breath

16. Finally, in that same movie (it was a genre breakthrough, after all), the zombies met their maker in what manner?

    a. They were crushed by the sugar-mill auger.

    b. They followed each other off the edge of a cliff (and I do not like the inferred lemming metaphor one little bit).

    c. As soon as Lugosi died, they did too. Drag.

    d. A good witchdoctor freed their souls and they flew away on invisible dragons.

17. What is a *bokor*?

    a. One who bokes.

    b. A voodoo sorcerer.

    c. A Nordic surname.

    d. One of Aquaman's archenemies.

18. The first film to actually feature a zombie speaking the word "brains" was?

    a. *House of the Living Dead*

    b. *Foreclosure of the Living Dead*

    c. *Eviction of the Living Dead*

    d. *Return of the Living Dead*

19. The nineties had a boatload of zombie films, a few of which were truly amazing. In my humble opinion, *Fido* was one of those. Who played Fido?

    a. Willem Dafoe

    b. Martin Lawrence

    c. Billy Connolly

    d. Cesar Milan

20. *Christine, Princess of Eroticism*, made in 1973, may be one of the crappiest movies ever. It goes by several other names—which of the selections below is *not* one of those?

    a. *A Virgin Among the Living Dead*

    b. *Eine Jungfrau in den Krallen von Zombies*

    c. *Among the Living Dead*

    d. *Debbie Does Zombies*

21. As discussed earlier, a number of zombie films from the 1930s and '40s had racist undertones. Why would that be?

  a. It was the era, pure and simple. African American characters were limited to caricature roles and consistently were cast as "help." We've come a long way since then. Now black men in fat suits are able to play heavy-set, bossy old women. *That's* progress.

  b. It was symbolism. The former slaves, the zombies—it was about making a comparison. The writers and directors were carving out bold statements about the culture of the era and the wrongs that were being perpetrated.

  c. Oh no, it was racism.

  d. And not only that, but women were strictly "damsels in distress." Damn men.

22. What's datura?

  a. It's the model name of a Kia sub-subcompact.

  b. It was that town in Georgia that got so Horde-y it had to be blowed up. I bought the pay-per-view; it was dope!

  c. It's a mystical powder/spice that can be bought in bulk at nearly any Quali-Ko™. It goes nicely with poultry and, if you ingest it, ya get higher than a fruit bat, once the blinding abdominal cramps subside.

  d. It's a type of leafy annual that is known to have hallucinogenic properties, some of them toxic. A powdered version of the plant was used in voodoo rituals to zombify people. Boo-yah!

23. Where is the aforementioned bokor most likely to place a trapped soul?

    a. In a spiffy Tupperware container.

    b. In a bottle and then, later, the bokor will do "soul shooters" with his shady accomplices.

    c. In a pleasant condominium complex with low HOAs so the soul doesn't financially get in over his/her head.

    d. In a clay jar.

24. Here's a stupid title: *The Grapes of Death*. Really? Yup, really. Internationally, it's also known by several other titles—pick the fake one below.

    a. *Le Raisins de le Mort*

    b. *Killer Wine!*

    c. *Pestizide—Stadt der Zombies*

    d. *The Raisins of Death*

25. The year 2010 saw a Japanese film lower the bar in all the right ways. It was called, *Kyonyu Doragon—onsen zonbi vs sutorippa 5*. For English speaking audiences it was renamed what? (I warned you this would be difficult.)

    a. *Zombies vs. Hot Oil Strippers*

    b. *The Big Tits Dragon*

    c. *Strippers vs. the Living Dead Dragon*

    d. *Undead and Undressed*

26. How many times does one get to have the words "reefer" and "zombies" in a movie title? With *Doctor S Battles the Sex-Crazed Reefer Zombies: The Movie,* we lucked out. In this film, what turns people into zombies?

   a. Sex

   b. Reefer

   c. Fox News

   d. Doctor S

27. The Zombies is a British band featuring Rod Argent and Colin Blunstone, who had quite a string of hits. Which one of these was *not* one of their songs?

   a. "She's Not There"

   b. "Time of the Season"

   c. "Mandy's Missing in the Marshes"

   d. "Hold Your Head Up"

"Go-o-o-o-o, Dead!"

28. What does the term "zombie bank" mean?

   a. It's a bank that's being run by the living dead, which doesn't make much sense. The tellers would be even less cooperative and any transaction would take too long. Bad idea.

   b. A financial institution that disperses organs, human or otherwise.

   c. A financial institution that has zero net worth, but can continue to operate based on governmental guarantees.

   d. A lovely hill adjacent to a river where zombies can go to relax and spend quiet time staring at the clouds.

29. Finish the title of this 1973 film: *Children Shouldn't Play with*

_____.

   a. *Ninjas*

   b. *Cobras and Would Be Wise to Avoid Boa Constrictors, Too*

   c. *Flame Throwers*

   d. *Dead Things*

30. A real stinker from last century is *Zombiez*, which claims to be part of a film genre called "hip-hop horror." The only good thing about this flick is it proves bad filmmaking isn't limited to white folk. In this doozy, the "zombiez" have weaponz they carry around and sometimes uze. What are they?

   a. Nerf gunz

   b. Large wooden clubz

   c. Hand-held sicklez

   d. Shivz

31. Norway entered the crap contest a few years back with *Død Snø* (which, not surprisingly, translates to "Dead Snow"). This film featured a unique category of zombie. What was it?

   a. Zømbie CPAs

   b. Zømbie Waitresses

   c. Zømbie Nazis

   d. Zømbie Day Care Wørkers

32. Certain practices of Haitian voodoo are closely related to what religion?

   a. Druidism

   b. Judaism

   c. Whaddya call it, the one with the folks at your door where you don't dare answer or they'll talk your damn ear off and try to give you a magazine. That one?

   d. Catholicism

33. The catchphrase for Germany's 1990 dubious entry, *Demon Wind*, was what?

   a. You smelt it, you dealt it.

   b. Whew! What did you eat last night?

   c. There's something deadly in the air.

   d. Somebody, open a window!

34. The movie *Hot Wax Zombies on Wheels*—why?

   a. There's a buck to be made.

   b. Zombies and bikers—hells, yeah!

   c. Why not? Lighten up—we're talkin' zombies!

   d. Some schmuck had a vision—let him be.

35. A couple of folks from Pittsburgh have created a zombie opera. Hooray! What's it called?

   a. *Aidead*

   b. *Rigormorto*

   c. *Evenings in Quarantine: The Zombie Opera*

   d. *Pagliacci Cacciatore: A Clown Casserole*

36. It would be a shame not to ask one more question about *Plan 9 From Outer Space*, doncha think? When the "film" (using the term loosely) was previewed, what was its different title?

a. *Plan 8 From Outer Space*

b. *So, You're Tellin' Me Lugosi Is Dead?!*

c. *Grave Robbers From Outer Space*

d. *Screamatorium*

37. "*Scooby-Doo on Zombie Island*, a direct-to-DVD release, despite what you might think, qualifies as an actual zombie film." Which answer below best supports or refutes that statement?

a. Scooby-Doo always sucked, still sucks, and the film was merely an attempt to capitalize on zombie culture. I can't and won't acknowledge it as being part of the genre. Never.

b. It's a lousy piece of animation (or should I say "re-animation"?) but still, it has zombies. Like it or not, it's in.

c. What's next—*Death of a Salesman* with a living dead Willy Loman? And we'd label that a zombie film too? Enough with all the madcap mash-ups already. I want my zombies to return to traditional values in a place where they actually belong— out in the woods or in the suburbs threatening innocents in metaphorical ways.

d. It's a cute way to introduce kids to zombies. So what if it's cheesy? As if all these other films are such works of art? Please. Stop treating the zombs like they're all *so* precious.

38. *Return of the Living Dead III*. Uh-huh. What actor, made famous by his TV portrayal of an LA cop, starred in this sequel to a sequel from a spin-off?

    a. Kent McCord

    b. Randolph Mantooth

    c. Jack Webb

    d. Harry Morgan

39. Apparently the French have their own issues about putting together a decent zombie movie. The plot of *The Oasis of the Living Dead* involves an evil treasure hunter going to the desert to look for what?

One of Columbus's early fascist ships.

    a. Water?

    b. Sand?

    c. Nazi gold?

    d. A better title for the film?

40. A female voodoo priest is called a _____?

    a. Hounganette

    b. Sally

    c. Mambo

    d. Samba

41. The very first organized zombie walk occurred in what city?

   a. Toronto

   b. Sacramento

   c. Whorlando

   d. Provo

42. E.S.C. and the Académie believe the living dead are, like Moab or Yellowstone, natural wonders and are capable of being valuable tourist attractions. Consequently, the idea of killing them really chafes their collective hide. However, they are aware that "survival" concepts appeal to a demographic with strong antisocial tendencies. So, to humor those folks, here goes—how does one *not* kill a zombie?

   a. Shoot 'em in the head, man—quick and easy.

   b. Trowel to the temple or a carrot through the heart.

   c. Don't even mess with that shit—chop the head clean off. Use a shovel or machete. Yeah, a machete. I *love* machetes!

   d. Make 'em watch *1,000 Ways to Die* on Spike TV. That'll take anyone out.

43. The translation of *coup de poudre* is what?

   a. Lipton Cup-A-Powder

   b. Proud chicken

   c. Powder strike

   d. Something about a rebellion

44. The German release of 1978's *Dawn of the Dead* was nearly a half hour longer than the American release. Why?

   a. Those Germans are hardcore.

   b. New subplot inserted with zombies shopping at a once-a-year event at Mervyn's.

   c. Additional carnage footage has been slo-mo'ed to a crawl.

   d. Less consumer symbolism/more gore.

45. Name the iconic porn star in the film *Zombie Strippers*.

   a. Jenna Jennason

   b. Jenna Jameson

   c. Jamie Jennason

   d. Jamie Jamerson

46. The Italians cranked out *Cemetery Man* in 1994. It starred what suave and hunky actor?

   a. Hugh Jackman

   b. Hugh Grant

   c. Rupert Everett

   d. Hugh Beaumont

47. What's *bufotoxin*?

   a. A poisonous secretion from kittens

   b. A lethal compound found only in the digestive tract of televangelists

   c. Toad venom

   d. The deadly pollen of the bufo flower

48. Who was one of the executive producers for the 1990 remake of *Night of the Living Dead*?

a. Tor Johnson

b. George Lucas

c. George Romero

d. George Jetson

49. In *Zombie Lake*, another winner from France, the zombies were a select group of humans who were purposely drowned. (And one can only imagine how awful a water-logged, pruney zombie would look.) These folks were whom?

a. Local French officials who had the nerve to demand that employees take on a 30-hour workweek.

b. People who'd worked at a nearby café that served inferior croissants and spoiled *fromage*.

c. Nazis (yet again) who'd been killed by the townspeople decades prior.

d. Aquatic living dead sommeliers.

50. Christopher Lee and Donald Sutherland somehow made their way into Italy's 1960s mess of a movie, *Castle of the Living Dead*. What's unusual about the directorial credit of this film?

a. It's the notorious Alan Smithee.

b. Three people are listed.

c. It's Fellini.

d. No director would take credit.

THE LIGHTNING ROUND

(THESE ARE FOR BONUS POINTS, SO THEY'RE TOUGHER, BITCHES.)

(Circle the correct answer.)

1. Legendary makeup artist Tom Savini has also worn other professional hats during his career. Circle the hat he has *not* worn.
   a. Stuntman
   b. Director
   c. Actor
   d. Cinematographer

2. Back in the 1930s, a fellow named George Terwilliger made what many experts consider to be the *second* full-length zombie film. That film was?
   a. *Zombie Forest*
   b. *Mora-gu!*
   c. *Ouanga*
   d. *Return of the Zombie*

3. The highest grossing zombie film ever is:
   a. *Dawn of the Dead* (2004)
   b. *Zombieland*
   c. *Titanic*
   d. *White Zombie* (adjusted for ticket price inflation)

4. Wes Craven directed what 1988 film based loosely on the real-life adventures of anthropologist Wade Davis?

   a. *Voodon't*

   b. *Nightmare on Mamba Avenue*

   c. *The Serpent and the Rainbow*

   d. *Love Bug 9: Herbie's Revenge*

5. In 1945's *Zombies on Broadway*, what popular actor played the heavy, Ace Miller? Hint: he would go on to produce *The Andy Griffith Show* and *The Dick Van Dyke Show*, among others.

   a. Carl Reiner

   b. Danny Thomas

   c. Sheldon Leonard

   d. Howard Sprague

"Boyle Face Institute? Yes, I can hold."

6. Ireland's National Zombie Day is when?

   a. October 30

   b. September 14

   c. August 1

   d. There is no National Zombie Day in Ireland. Duh.

7. Finish the quote and name the movie: "When there's no more room in hell, the dead shall walk the _____."

   a. Mall/*Zombie Academy 4*

   b. Plank/*Zombie Pirates Ahoy*

   c. Line/*Johnny Cash—Dead from San Quentin*

   d. Earth/*Dawn of the Dead*

8. "A member of the Horde has no sense of its own actions." Choose the best answer agreeing or disagreeing with this statement.
   a. Agreed. They're in first gear *and* on autopilot.
   b. Incorrect. There's a primal sense of survival and most experts agree that this infers self-awareness.
   c. Neither agree nor disagree. There's not enough evidence to know either way.
   d. Who cares? I just want to shoot one—it's on my bucket list. Next time I find a free-ranger out stumblin' around, that's exactly what I'm gonna do. I'm gonna mess him up real good. Then we'll see what kind of awareness the sumbitch has.

9. What method of infection is the least painful?
   a. A little bite on the finger
   b. Tainted Hemo-Glowin™ transfusion
   c. Stealing a kiss from a Horde member
   d. "Bobbin' for Blowfish Night" at the Elks Lodge

10. If George Bernard Shaw had written a zombie play, it would've been called _____.
    a. *Babe the Pygmalion*
    b. *Androcles and the Lion King*
    c. *No Arms and the Man*
    d. *Augustus Does His Bit but Does Not Make the Top 24*

11. In *Planet Terror*, zombies have a different moniker. What is it?

  a. Lance

  b. Sickos

  c. Pukes

  d. Walkers

12. What is George Romero's middle name?

  a. Ringo

  b. Wallace

  c. Andrew

  d. Alan

INTERROGATION

When ready, close your Exam, put your pencil down, and push the green button. The Proctors will let the Examiners know it's time. Try not to crap yourself.

A COMMENCEMENT ADDRESS

FROM YOUR PRESIDENT,
President Dutch Bingo

Let me be the first person to congratulate you on getting through your Zombie Exam. I'm sure it wasn't easy. I should know—I've flunked it three times. Of course, being Your President means I'm not allowed to participate in the Interrogation section of the test. And that's a shame because I could so nail the Interrogation and take whatever those Examiner wienies would dish out. Little known fact: I've got very punchable abs.

On a glorious graduation day such as this, I reflect back on my predecessor, Dirk Manley, your former president and world-class bodybuilder, God rest his soul. I believe he would've looked out over this crowd of eager and happy faces and said, "What the *hell* are you smiling about? You haven't done squat." He was a softie like that.

Former Pres. Manley in his younger years.

As for me, here's my take on your achievement: now that you're about to attain this degree, do yourself and everyone else a favor—don't gloat. I'm always disappointed when I see Ph.Z. grads getting uppity about their sheepskin and waving it around like it's a first edition Jackie Collins novel. Yes, you've done well and we're all proud of you, but enough with the "Whooo hoooos" and "Take ZAT" talk. As I like to say, "Don't put the 'dip' in diploma." Even if you *are* a colossal maroon, act like you've been there before. If not, with a snap of my fingers I could dial up all sorts of surly operatives who'd be happy to make your life a living hell simply because I asked them to. Or, I could always arrange to have you bitten; that would shut your ass up.

Rather than wasting your energy on pathetic self-aggrandizement, go out and do something that will help others. The best graduates are not interested in simply appearing to be cool, they're more about *being* cool—having a big heart and all that altruistic crap. I'll have you know, years ago, I spent ten summer days before my junior year in college chatting about addiction with clients at a local shelter. We even pounded down a few Olde English 800s when no one was looking. And yes, for the sake of full disclosure,

Sit the hell down, Jimmy. No one wants to hear you brag about the Exam anymore.

the experience was court-mandated, but still, I was there and I remember how deeply I touched their lives.

Let's face it—this world is totally hosed right now and our country will surely fall farther into that hosey mess if we all don't pitch in. So, take what you've learned from the ZAT and move forward with grace in your heart, a sense of love for your fellow man, and a small caliber handgun in case you get in a pickle.

Also, you might recommend the Zombie Exam to your friends. And by "friends" I don't mean people you met once at a mall and then "friended" on a social network site whose ads seem to think you might enjoy pork-flavored mayonnaise. I mean genuine friends—people you talk to and share experiences with *in person*. Remember "in person"? That's different than video chatting with someone. You understand that, right?

Anyway, I'm betting you know a dunderhead or three. If so, encouraging them to take the Exam would be a generous act. No, no—stop texting. Regale them with your inspirational and educational success story the next time you gather for lunch or something like that. *In person.* Okay? Dang.

And please look for my latest memoir, *Profiles in Sewage: From the Brink and Back*, co-written with my dear friend and colleague, Dr. Kenneth Beaker. Inside you'll find a real page-turner with stories about everything from how far our country has come since the Disaster to a hilarious anecdote about how I once almost bombed Scotland. Whew—that was close! *Profiles in*

"Oh, that Bingo is such a wonderful writer!"

Sewage is available wherever you still might find remaining bookstores and, of course, on the Tubes.

So gather ye diplomas, oh scholars, and make us all proud! Lift up thine eyes to the skies of the future and do good, or, at a minimum, try not to make things worse. You represent humanity—if we wanted to hang out with idiots, we'd visit a Containment Zone.

And aim high because, if you don't, I *will* make that call to the operatives. They're itching for an assignment like you. Got it?

God Bless.

Your President,
President Dutch Bingo

The Capon Académie of Port-Au-Prince

Upon the recommendation of some guy,

The Capon Académie does hereby proudly confer upon

....

(Your Name—and try to write nicely. This is a big deal for you.)

the degree of

Ph.Z. — Philosopher of Zombieology

And all the cool stuff appertaining thereto.

In witlessness whereof, the seal of the Académie, and the signatures as authorized by the Bored of Directors of Exam Services Corporation and the Académie are offered hereto,

this .... day of ...., in the year ....

Go forth and groove!

The Capon Académie
of Port-Au-Prince
We learned you good!

Dr. Kenneth Beaker
DR. KENNETH BEAKER

X
CHOMPS THE CLOWN

(Waring: do NOT duplicate. Fasza, the high priest, is all over this piracy thing and you sooooo do not want to piss him off. The last person that did is still working to get her speech skills back.)

LEGAL DISCLAIMER

All information contained in this book is for informational purposes only and not for any actual educational use. How could you possibly think otherwise? The Capon Académie and Exam Services Corporation in no way guarantee any value regarding the diploma or opportunities that might come about as a result of getting said diploma. Don't go griping to us if you don't experience a major transformation in your life—no one promised you anything.

The opinions expressed in the book were those of the harebrained author and not of the Capon Académie or Exam Services Corporation. We're way hipper than he is.

Additionally, nothing contained in this disclaimer negates a lot of the dandy content herein, nor should it discourage you from pursuing the Ph.Z. Plus Program found on the following page.

NOW THAT YOU'VE ACHIEVED THIS "DEGREE" OF SUCCESS, WHY STOP HERE?

"I think I'm headin' for the Platinum Level, Jimmy."

With only a bit more effort and a not inconsiderable additional financial burden, you could advance your cause even further. Exam Services Corporation now presents the Ph.Z. Plus Program featuring the Silver, Gold, and Platinum levels! Why would you settle for living on the second story when you could move up to a penthouse? Cool fact: people look like ants from a penthouse and, quite frankly, most look better as a result.

We'd like to tell you more about the Ph.Z. Plus Program right now, but certain restrictions and unsettled lawsuits in multiple remaining states prevent us from doing so. But, if you call 1-866-PHZPLUS, one of our qualified operators will be somewhat

"Exam Services Corp.? Yes, I can hold."

happy to speak with you concerning this additional step forward in your educational future.

So, give us a call and let's see what we can do for you.

Remember, "We'll learn you good!"

ANSWERS

Answers? You really want answers to the Exam? Huh.

A diploma isn't enough? Overachiever.

Go to www.zombiesforzombies.com.

I've got your answers—right here!

Appendix A:
....

TESTING THROUGH THE AGES!

∙∙∙
∙∙∙

(This article first appeared in the September 2008 issue of
Testing Monthly and is used here by permission.)

"Know your enemy," they say, whoever the hell they are. In this case, the enemy is an exam. Let's see how far our testing civilization has come. Sound fun? Of course not.

THE REALLY, REALLY, REALLY EARLY YEARS.

A couple of autumns ago, the world's oldest test was discovered on an archaeological dig outside a strip mall in Baltimore. Scientists estimate that the granite tablets found were used somewhere between the Greek and Flinstonian eras. What was preserved of the original test documentation informs us of the futility of early test takers. Apparently hammers and chisels weren't the most efficient way to record answers back then. This would explain why an entire week was set aside for tests and the related remarkably high dropout rate. As for chiseling an essay, don't even start.

Later, after the invention of the stick, students found they had the ability to write answers in dirt. This came to be viewed as only a minor leap forward due to the drawback of strong winds, precipitation, and the fact that each completed test took up half an acre.

THE MIRACLE OF PAPER.

Finally, a type of primitive paper was invented, made from papyrus. This was a huge step forward and resulted in the genesis of direct mail marketing.

"Great Odin's beard, Bob! What kind of godforsaken paper is this?"

Millions of years went by and paper evolved, this time into a product made from wood. "Timberrrr!"—the logging industry was born along with *Ax-Men.* The world-changing creation of mass-produced paper ignited a revolution in how we were able to communicate with one another. People were stunned to find they could actually *record their thoughts*, preserve their childish poetry, or write naughty letters to *Penthouse.*

As writing became more commonplace, tests also evolved and soon became more palatable to the user and more productive for the test giver.

And once paper was easily obtainable, the idea emerged that, if it was softened a little, it would be better for our butts than leaves or corncobs.

NOT EVERYONE DEPENDED ON THE WRITTEN WORD.

Throughout history, certain cultures decided to forgo written exams because, in their limited society, paper was scarce and the nearest Office Depot was nineteen-hundred years away. This left the local test givers to pursue two other courses: (1) the "doing" exam and (g) the oral exam.

The doing exam was, by far, the most popular (and one we can't recreate here—too chaotic). For example, it has been noted that the Huns put all recruits through mandatory final trials. In order to achieve the levels of proficiency needed for various Hunnic skills, these tests were divided into four parts: archery, metallurgy, pillaging, and dessert making. (Despite being a foul-smelling swamp people, the Huns were, nonetheless, known throughout their conquered lands for making beautiful pastries and puddings.) Hun students who did not achieve a passing score were given the choice of being exiled from their homeland or killed, thus leading to a tremendous amount of cramming and packing on the eve of trials.

DID YOU KNOW?

Gutenberg is best known for his Bible, but I bet you weren't aware that he printed other pieces, too. He dabbled in pamphlets and did business cards for a few close friends. And he printed the first phone book, which was blank because the phone hadn't been invented.

Another curious version of the doing test was demonstrated in the mid-18th century by the Maknak tribe of southern Africa. When a boy was deemed to have reached puberty, he was sent out alone into the wilderness to prove his manhood. Once there, he could return to the village only after he'd killed a gazelle, found a new water source, and mated with a neighboring tribal chick. Upon his return, the entire tribe would celebrate by feasting on gazelle and water, and would nervously avoid asking him about how it went with the chick. Interestingly, there were no like-minded tests for the adolescent women of the Maknak—girls were instead encouraged to develop home-based businesses, work on their nails, and give in to the males' disgusting advances.

Meanwhile, language began to replace flash cards in the ancient world and the oral exam quickly gained in popularity. As cultures became more fluent in their own tongues and people could "understand" one another, certain groups began to migrate from "doing" to "talking." This was not all bad, except for the town talkers from the Trump province of northern England. Their exhausting diatribes led to the invention of "shhhhhh."

This doing/talking shift took a turn for the worse when people began to, rather than do, simply *talk* about doing, which led to nothing getting done. Oddly, those folks still felt great about themselves. (Think Hollywood or DC.)

THE MODERN AGE AND "EXTRA CREDIT."

In the years that followed the end of WWII, many countries put forth an effort to be perkier and show gratitude for the fact that they hadn't had the shit bombed out of them. In order to boost the collective morale of their citizenry and get a more educated workforce back in place, governments encouraged educators to cut the students slack. One of the ways that this was accomplished was by the invention of "extra credit."

In the spring of 1949, the first evidence of extra credit surfaced on a Driver's Ed exam in Oslo. Here's how it worked: any person who missed one too many questions on the test got a chance to write a paragraph about why it was important that he or she keep driving *or* they could watch a 30-minute presentation about ice fishing. Either choice would negate the one wrong answer and the student would be on their way, with license in hand.

When word of this crazy extra-credit concept reached the rest of the world, businesses were quick to adopt it. Why, even television got into the act by introducing the "Lightning Round," wherein contestants would gain a chance at additional cash and prizes. Interestingly, the first true Lightning Round was introduced to the world via a 1959 game show on NBC called—wait for it—"Extra Credit." Wild.

THE COMING OF THE INTERNET AND THE FUTURE OF TESTING.

And so we return to the present, to a world where the miracle of the Internet is transforming our test-filled lives on a daily basis. Through the billions of miles of cables and wires that require a cord bundler the size of the St. Louis Arch, all sorts of useless information is passed between our homes and businesses at dizzying speeds. This innovation has created tremendous innovations including:

"Hello, Operator? Please connect me to the future."

- ⊙ "Virtual classrooms" where avatar students interact with avatar teachers in a pretend auditorium. Such an educational environment does a remarkable job of approximating the stultifying feel of a real classroom. This technological breakthrough is called "distance learning," which allows students from all over the world to take courses in nearly any subject without having to worry about transportation or personal hygiene. Not only does this cost-effective tool cut back on the cribbing of info from student to student, but it also minimizes the risk of troubled, middle-aged instructors of both sexes leering at their succulent, wide-eyed students.

- The option to apply for a job online gives users the opportunity to seek employment from the comfort of their homes and to wonder why they use such an outdated browser. The advantage here is employers aren't subjected to the 92.7 percent of applicants who are either not qualified or barely functional. And for the employee-not-to-be, the emotional investment is lessened due to the lack of interaction. Consequently, another failed attempt to land that great job won't be quite as depressing. Furthermore, the green factor here is undeniable—less paperwork and fewer stolen packs of Post-Its. For those proud few who make it past the initial application, the online interview can prove daunting. Here are a few simple tips: stare directly into your webcam and try not to blink excessively (no need to go all "Steve Forbes" during it, though), close all porn windows before the interview, and, lastly, remember to wear pants—just because you'll be seen from the waist up is no reason not to behave appropriately. What if there's an emergency and you have to run from the monitor? That wouldn't look good, would it?

Futurists like the dazzling Mr. Tony Stark tell us that what's on the horizon will be even more compelling:

- The Testy—a full-blown testing body suit (with goggles) that will enable you, via the Net, to immerse yourself directly into your virtual classroom, interview, or what have you. This incredible tech-schmatta puts you and your bod right in the thick of any sort of activities that are better when not experienced in person. And all of this can be done from the comfort of your home, your Barcalounger, your lawn chair, or— oh yeah—your bed. That's what I'm talkin' about!

"If I don't get at least a 'B' on my Voodoo mid-term, I'm screwed."

⊙ Virtual College Exams—no more pencils, no more books, no more teachers. Since students will no longer have to show up at brick-and-mortar institutions, teachers won't be needed to supervise. And once that weekend overtime disappears off the payroll of our greedy educators, the savings will be huge for the overburdened budgets of our communities and their nearly bankrupt schools. Win/win!

⊙ Virtual voting—because of this breakthrough technology, the inability to darken a dot or punch a hole through a flimsy card will no longer be an embarrassment. With a mere click, citizens will be able to elect whomever they please—at least until their computer freezes and produces what's known in the IT world as a "virtual chad."

As you can see, from yesterday to tomorrow, testing has been and will continue to be a key element in the ongoing progress of our civilization. Go forth and groove!

LASTLY—

The country of Haiti continues to struggle after a massive
7.0 earthquake struck on January 12, 2010.

Haiti has been shown a lot of love from zombie
fans and creators over the decades.

Please consider showing a little more.

Donations can be made through these websites, among others:

www.unicef.org

www.care.org

www.redcross.org

www.mercycorps.org

www.savethechildren.org

www.jphro.org

www.clintonbushhaitifund.org

Thank you.

ABOUT THE AUTHOR

David P. Murphy is the author of *Zombies for Zombies: Advice and Etiquette for the Living Dead* and *Zombies for Zombies—The Play and Werk Buk*.

David is also a songwriter and producer of three CDs, *Shining in a Temporary Sun*, Henry Perry's *Effortless*, and Camille Metoyer Moten's *A Simpler Christmas*. His next album, *My Fraudulent Memoir*, will be released in the fall of 2011.

Murphy has been playing piano since he was a kid and is still trying to get it right.

After twenty-five years in Los Angeles, David now resides in his hometown of Omaha, Nebraska. He has recently completed his newest musical, *anotherwhere*.

For more information about David, please see www.youtube.com/Z4Zbook, www.zombiesforzombies.com, or www.davidpmurphy.com.

NOTES:

....

....

....

....

....

....

....

....

....

....

....

....

....

....

NOTES:

....

....

....

....

....

....

....

....

....

....

....

....

....

....

NOTES:

....

....

....

....

....

....

....

....

....

....

....

....

....

....

NOTES:

....

....

....

....

....

....

....

....

....

....

....

....

....

....

....

NOTES:

....

....

....

....

....

....

....

....

....

....

....

....

....

....

NOTES:

....
....
....
....
....
....
....
....
....
....
....
....
....
....
....

NOTES:

....

....

....

....

....

....

....

....

....

....

....

....

....

....

NOTES:

....
....
....
....
....
....
....
....
....
....
....
....
....
....
....

ZOMBIES FOR ZOMBIES
ADVICE AND ETIQUETTE FOR THE LIVING DEAD

So, you've been bitten by a zombie? Bummer. But there's no need to panic! *Zombies for Zombies* is a motivational guide designed specifically to make a profound difference in your accidental, strange new life.

ZOMBIES FOR ZOMBIES—THE PLAY AND WERK BUK
THE WORLD'S BESTSELLING INACTIVITY GUIDE FOR THE LIVING DEAD

The best games for your brainz (for thinkin', not eatin'). Just when you thought brains couldn't get any more appealing, *Zombies for Zombies— The Play and Werk Buk* gives you, a recently turned zombie, a treasure trove of games, puzzles, stories, quizzes, and other fun ways to embrace and improve your new zombie life.